Pretty
FOR A CRIPPLED
Girl

A MEMOIR ON
DISABILITY & MOBILITY

TERI
SIRI

NewSage Press
Oregon

Pretty for a Crippled Girl

Paperback Original ISBN 978-0-939165-84-1
Hardcover, Library Edition ISBN 978-0-939165-85-8
EBook ISBN 978-0-939165-86-5

NewSage Press
P.O. Box 611
Tillamook, OR 97141
www.newsagepress.com

Cover & Book Design by Sherry Wachter
MagicDogPress.com
Printed in the United States
Distributed by Publishers Group West

Library of Congress Cataloging-in-Publication Data
Siri, Teri Ann, 1964-

For Those Who

Knew I Could Do It

"If you are comfortable with my oppression, then you are my oppressor."

A. Philip Randolph
American Civil Rights
& Labor Leader

Contents

Acknowledgments

This book has been on my mind for decades. It's finally here, and ready for all to read. Without the support and encouragement of many people, I couldn't have done this.

My parents, grandparents, sisters, aunts, uncles, cousins, nieces and nephews have been a source of ongoing support as well as constant teasing in my life. I have always felt their love and encouragement. And when I began talking about writing a book, they cheered me on and now celebrate my accomplishment. I am especially grateful to Aunt Carol and Uncle Gary for always opening their home and hearts to me when I visited Portland, and providing hours of quiet when I had long meetings with my publisher at their kitchen table.

For my lifelong friends, Kelly, Joanie, and Cindy—thank you for years of laughter, great memories, and true friendship. You've always had my best interests in mind, and I appreciate your honesty when I needed to hear it. Even if it wasn't easy to hear at times, I know you were coming from a good place; that's what real friends do. I am so grateful I met each of you when I most needed a true friend. Your friendships have made all the difference.

I am grateful for my work friends, who have encouraged me for years to write this book, and now are so excited to see it become real. The best part of working at BPA was the people I met. A special shout out to Mary B, who passed away in 2025. Mary was witty and fun-loving from day one at work.

Romantic loves in my life, which I once thought would not be possible, did happen. They all taught me I am worthy of love, even when I wasn't sure it was possible or when it was challenging. My former husband, Joel, and I will always be friends. I am proud of, and thankful for, this special man.

To my love today, Claus, for his love and support and constant quips, which have been some version of: "Write your fucking book. You have something to say." Even during the times when I wanted to give up on my book, Claus's nagging words of encouragement would be lurking around in the back of my mind. Claus is Bavarian, and according to him, Bavarians are not known for soft edges. So, thank you Claus for not mincing words. I appreciate your directness, but I love your softness most. Get ready for the next adventure!

My editor and publisher, Maureen R. Michelson, was also a counselor and a motivator. She understood my message from the start, she heard what I was saying: I do not want to be anyone's inspiration. I just want to show I live my life just like "normal" people. Thank you, Maureen, with every ounce of my being for getting that message across. Along the way, we have become friends, and I am happy for our friendship. How could we not be after years of working together to bring this book to life? And because of Maureen, my book designer, Sherry Wachter, helped bring my story to life with a "spot on" book cover that captures my love of adventure. I am grateful for her design talents to make this book visually beautiful and professional.

The stars in my life, Robert and Millie Goldsmith, my grandparents, Nana and Bapa, and their love and encouragement are the threads that run throughout this book. I miss them every day and I still talk about them regularly because everyone should have had the pleasure of knowing them. They were the best influences in my life, and their humor and unconditional love have meant everything to me. Without them, my life would have paled and perhaps this book wouldn't have seen the light of day. I am sad they aren't here to read my memoir, but their memory lives on in these pages. Thank you, Nana and Bapa!

Pretty

FOR A CRIPPLED

Girl

Teri (left) with Traci, Tami, and their mom, Cheryl.

Chapter 1

A Vegetable? Or a Wild Life?

The first story I remember hearing—and I heard it repeatedly throughout my life—was the one about the woman from an organization for crippled children who showed up at my mom's door. The message was dire. She made a declaration about my future: "This child will be a vegetable for the rest of her life."

That prediction was the beginning of my roller-coaster life with cerebral palsy (CP). Fortunately, Mom didn't listen to the doctors—she kept me. As it turned out, I didn't become a vegetable, but instead, I continue to live a full, productive, and sometimes wild, life. Of course, after that mystery woman's dead wrong prediction, my grandma, Nana Millie, was sure to not donate money to that organization. And Mom, from then on, made it clear she never cared much for the Oregon social workers. As for me, I surpassed the vegetable prediction and everyone else's expectations, so I'm relieved!

Something Is Wrong

Mom had turned 20 just a month before my sister and I were born in September 1964 in Portland, Oregon. We were about three months premature, and our skin was unusually dark at birth due to a lack of oxygen. Traci weighed 3.6 pounds, and I weighed 3.3 pounds. The doctors gave us 72 hours to live.

In those days, care for premature babies was a new field in medicine and the doctors were unsure of what to expect in our situation. After we passed the first critical period in those first three days and we were still alive, the doctors kept us in incubators for six weeks before Mom was allowed to bring us home.

My mom and dad had been in high school together but were never really sweethearts. However, Mom graduated in June 1962, and shortly after high school, they married. Within the first year, my older sister, Tami, was born in 1963. About one-and-a-half years later, my sister and I came along.

My dad was at the hospital when we were born, but soon after, they divorced, and he moved to California. He told my mom he wasn't ready for "daddyhood." In truth, I don't think either one of my young parents was ready for parenting. So, Dad left, and Mom became a single divorced mother of three young daughters, and one of us—me—would soon be considered "vegetable material."

At times, Mom held more than one job to support us. To put it mildly, she had her hands full, but fortunately, her parents, Nana and Bapa, lived nearby and they were an enormous help. Besides, big sister Tami loved taking care of "her babies." Mom said Tami was so happy to have two new babies to care for!

Years later, Mom told me that at first, the doctors thought my twin, Traci, was the unhealthiest of the two of us. But over time, it became obvious that I wasn't meeting developmental milestones like Traci's. My mom noticed I wasn't sitting up like Traci; I would just tip over. When Nana bathed me, I stiffened up. Something was wrong, so Mom took me for further medical examinations.

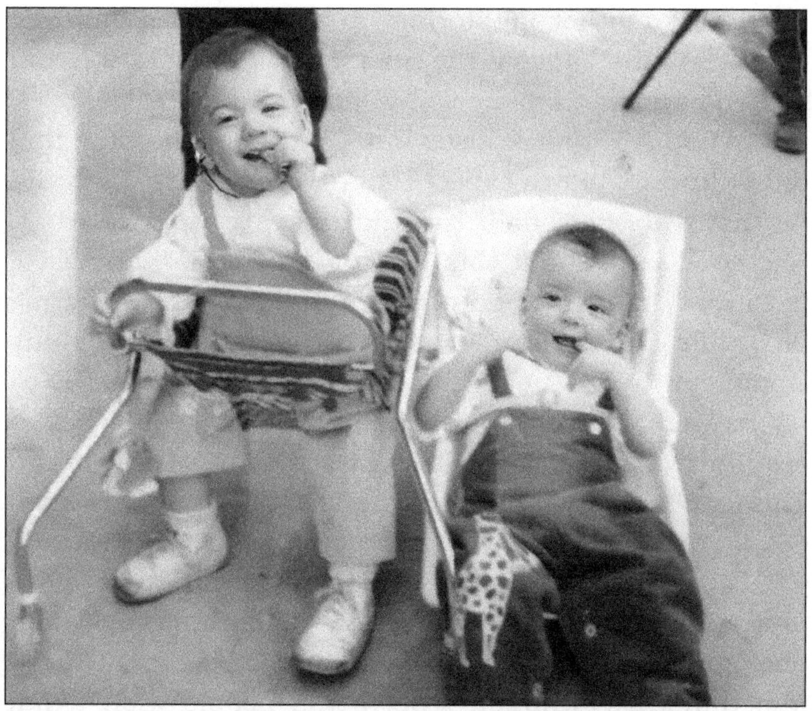

Teri (right) and Traci, about nine months old.

Cerebral Palsy

When I was about nine months old, the doctors diagnosed me with CP. They told Mom and Nana that I should be put in a home for children with physical disabilities. According to Mom, the doctor said, "Your baby has cerebral palsy." Then he matter-of-factly added, "She won't amount to much."

Little else was said that day in the doctor's office. Mom took me home, stunned by the news. She cried most of the way, alone and uncertain what to do. Many years later, she admitted to me that on the ride home from the doctor's appointment, she thought about driving into the side of a bridge! In that moment, it all felt too overwhelming for her, especially because she knew nothing about CP. When I think of that, I imagine my young mother mustering up some kind of amazing courage to just stay on the road, keep driving home, and somehow trust that she would find a way.

My family didn't know what CP was at the time and didn't know what to expect. They weren't sure if I would be just a drooler, or if I would talk, or walk, or what. The good part about this lack of information about CP is that my mom and grandparents didn't hover over me or coddle me. As I grew, they expected me to do many things for myself.

In time, my family learned CP is a disability that results from damage to the gray matter of the brain. This can happen before, during, or shortly after birth. CP is different for everyone who has it. Outwardly, CP is manifested by muscular incoordination and/or speech disturbances. From the beginning, my main challenges were my legs and walking. I never had speech impediments, although I bet some people wish I did, since I've heard many complaints for what comes out of my mouth! I tend to speak my mind loudly and clearly—especially if I'm passionate about something. More on that, later.

After consulting with several doctors, Mom took me to another specialist when I was about nine months old. He talked with Mom about the first steps needed to straighten my legs. In the middle of the office visit, a nurse took me from my mother and left the room. A short time later, she brought me back and I had plaster leg casts up to my waist. When Mom saw me in those leg casts, she cried, shocked at the sight of her small baby in such a huge cast. This was the first of many procedures and surgeries to correct my legs so I could crawl and eventually, walk.

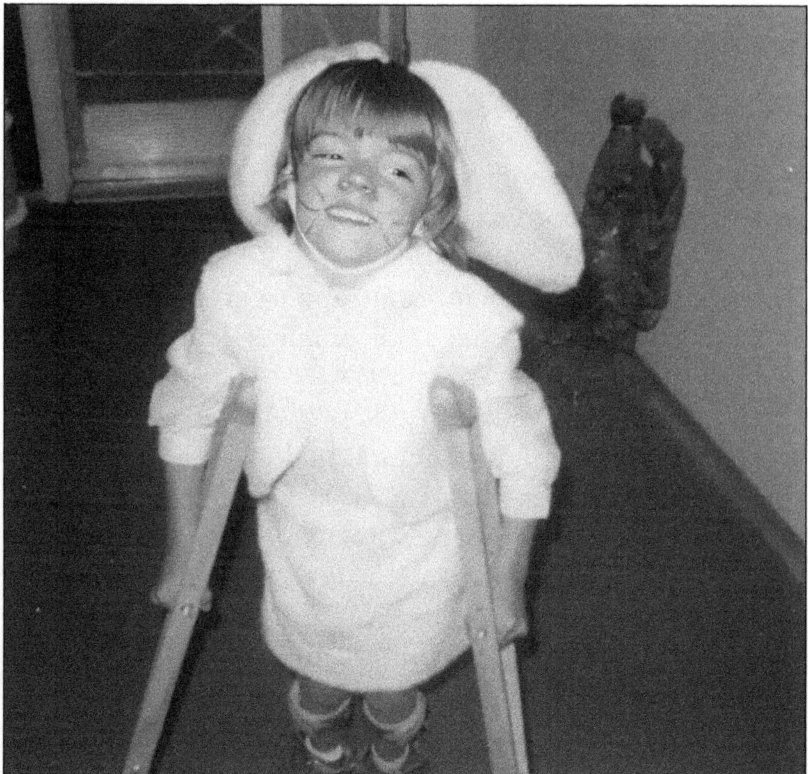

Teri in her Halloween costume.

First, I Crawl

Sometime during my toddler years, Nana taught me to crawl, which was a big deal since I was not meeting my developmental milestones. The story I heard about learning to crawl was that one day Mom came home from work and Nana announced that I could crawl. She proceeded to show my mom how I crawled across the living room. Nana put me down on the floor and manually moved my limbs in a crawling motion, so I would understand the feeling. Once I got the movement down, then she enticed me with things I wanted. I had to crawl toward her while she waved the desired object in front of me. Nana said teaching me didn't take long. For years, crawling was my main mode of transport when I was home, and even as late as the sixth grade when I was able to walk with quad canes. When I crawled, I could quickly zoom all over the house.

My earliest memory is learning to use little wooden crutches with brown leather armbands to help me walk. About three years old, I had to slip my hands down through brown leather straps to grab the handles and slowly take steps. The whole experience was uncomfortable.

I had to wear a football helmet when I was outside because I was regularly falling, cracking my head open, and getting stitches. Imagine a young kid on crutches wearing a football helmet. Already, I was so aware of people staring at me when I walked with my crutches, and then when I started wearing a football helmet, the stares were off the chart. My memory tells me either the football-helmet phase was short lived, thankfully, or I was in some serious denial just to get through that awkward phase.

Is Your Twin Normal?

From an early age, people have asked about my twin, curious if she had CP. Or, as they liked to say, "Is she normal?"

When we were little, Traci used to ask Mom, "Why can't Teri walk, and I can?"

To this day, people often ask me, "Is your twin normal?"

When I hear that, I ask myself, *Who is normal? What is normal?*

I think I am normal. Other people don't see me that way, but I have always seen myself as normal.

From my perspective, it seems as if my twin has had a harder time reconciling why she is able to walk normally, and I have had to face numerous operations and deal with the challenges of CP. I always tell her, “Don’t worry about it, Traci,” but she does.

Perhaps this is why Traci has been my biggest protector, and I know she will defend me like no one else.

During those first years, Mom raised us with lots of help from my two favorite people in the world, my maternal grandparents, Nana and Bapa. Throughout my childhood we moved often, but my grandparents were always there for us. They were a tremendous support to Mom, and a deep source of love and support for their grandkids.

Everyone was surprised that I survived and thrived. “I had no idea how strong and smart you would become,” Mom admitted years later, recounting that time.

Sisters' bath time at Nana's house.

Chapter 2

Long Hospital Stays

Around four years old, we lived in Eugene, Oregon, and Mom enrolled me in Shriners Hospital School, also known as Pearl Buck School. This was an unusual school in 1968, started by Lisl Waechter, a special education teacher who had fled Nazi Germany in the 1940s. She settled in Oregon where she founded a private school for children with disabilities. Waechter asked Pulitzer Prize winning author Pearl S. Buck's permission to name the school after her because Buck had a daughter with developmental disabilities. Later, the school's name was changed to the Pearl Buck Center, and today, the center continues to help many children and adults with intellectual and developmental disabilities.

The Hospital, My Second Home

While we lived in Eugene, I spent a lot of time at Shriners Hospital for Crippled Children in Portland, where I had the first of many operations to help correct my legs. I was a regular patient and my story was familiar to many on the hospital staff. So, when I was five, I was named Oregon's Easter Seal child of 1969. They featured me in a local newspaper article as part of their fundraising efforts. In the caption under my photo, the media described me as a "cerebral palsy victim," which certainly reflected the judgments in those days toward people with disabilities.

Doctors operated on my legs several times to straighten them out, which included fusing my ankles so they were straight. On the weekends, Mom drove to Portland in her blue VW Beetle, my sisters in tow, to visit me at the hospital. In the 1960s, the hospital was called Shriners Hospital for Crippled Children. Now, it's the more politically correct Shriners Hospital for Children. My hospital stays could be for weeks at a time, and I slept in a big, ward-type room where beds were lined up next to each other. The linoleum floors were institutional black-and-white checkered squares. When I think of that place today, it reminds me of the orphanage scenes in the movie, *The Cider House Rules.*

In those days, my sisters were not allowed to visit my hospital room because they were too young. So, they sat outside on the lawn, looked up to my hospital window that had a crisscross pattern in the glass, and we chatted via walkie-talkies. Tami and Traci told me about what they did every day at home, but this kind of news just made me frustrated, lonely, and jealous. I'd get mad and cry and throw things on the floor, but mostly, I cried.

The whole hospital scene quickly became tiresome, and I resented not getting to be with my sisters at home. I was so young, and the hospital stays were so long—I missed my family terribly and I didn't understand why I couldn't just go home. Constantly, I asked my mom, "Are you going to take me home today?"

Whenever I asked, she didn't answer me. Instead, Mom just changed the subject and asked me things like, "What did you have for lunch today?"

But I just kept asking in my high-pitched, little girl's voice, "Will you take me home with you? I want to go home with you."

I can only imagine how this tugged at my mom's heart.

My Lifeline, a Tape Recorder

Sometimes, my mom brought tape-recorded messages from my sisters so I could hear their voices clearly, not through a garbled walkie talkie. They'd even sing songs for me. Often, their songs were made-up stories in which they'd call me "little princess." As a young kid, I found the tape recorder to be a magical box with blinking red lights that let me hear my sisters' voices. Mom encouraged me to send a message back to Traci and Tami. Fascinated, I'd timidly speak into the recorder, staring at the blinking red light: "I think I miss you and I want you to come in the hospital and push me on my bed," I told them. "I talk to you in the walkie-talkie when Mommy brings you down, when it's not a school day."

More than 50 years later, I still have those tape recordings. When I listen to those tapes now, I am still emotional because I sound so little and confused about why I had to stay in the hospital for so long. And if I see children today with disabilities, I am overcome with so many emotions. Loneliness and feeling like I am missing out on life experiences are feelings I dislike the most, to this day. I hate not being included in things, and I'm sure a shrink would say it stems from my childhood and long hospital stays.

Now, I understand that these hospital ordeals were hard on my family, too. Years later, Mom told me it broke her heart whenever I asked her to take me home from the hospital and she couldn't. They felt helpless seeing me go through struggles and pain that you wouldn't wish on anybody. On those tapes, there are lots of messages from my sisters in their own child voices, offering me encouragement. They said things like, "Teri, after this operation you will be able to run around and play with us."

On one of the tapes from May 1970, I am talking to my mom during a long hospital stay at Shriners Hospital in San Francisco. In my high-pitched, five-year-old voice, I asked Nana Millie, "When are you coming down? Will you and Mommy, Nana Great, and my daddy, come down and see me tomorrow?"

Then I asked, "Nana Millie, can I have a mustang horsey for all of us, for my present? I'll be able to ride it real good. Then my feet won't fall off because I have a cast on."

In that same recording, I told them about my friend Mary who also was staying at the hospital. "Mary's sisters are mean to her and they pick on her." Then Mom asked me a leading question about my own sisters. "Aren't you glad you have good sisters?"

"I'm glad I got good sisters that take care of me because they love me, and they miss me and...." Then I started to cry and added through my tears, "I miss them, too!"

During that same hospital stay, my older sister, Tami, sent me a taped message. "At school, my teacher gots a tape recorder just like this one and we get to turn it off and it says, stop the recorder. What are you doing? Oh, that's nice. (Laughs). Um, I love you. I hope you learn how to walk. Goodbye."

Then my twin, Traci, chimed in, "Teri, I hope tomorrow you learn how to walk and then you can come back and see your new house and then you can run all over in the patio with us. Teri, we love you, um, so much as big as the sky, and we miss you. Ok."

Two neighbor kids piped up and in their sweet voices added, "Goodbye princess. See you real soon."

For weeks at a time, these recordings were my only contact with my family and friends. There were many silly meandering messages about what each of us did that day, or what I ate for lunch, or who my sisters played with. They'd sing to me, and I sang to them. My sisters asked to use my coloring book, or I asked them how my tricycle was doing. With my mom's prompting, I'd thank my family for the gifts they sent during my hospital stay.

After that hospital visit, Nana did buy me the rocking horse; not the real thing, but that helped a little bit.

During another hospital stay, I went on a hunger strike because I was so sick and tired of being in the hospital. I refused to eat anything. The nurses told my mom if I didn't start eating by day three, they were going to put me on an I.V. for nourishment. Well, it was Bapa who got me to eat. All he said was, "Teri, do you want some chocolate ice cream?"

"Yes!" I said without a moment's hesitation.

That's all it took. I have always loved ice cream and Bapa knew it. Of course, he liked ice cream as much as I did, so he was interested in eating ice cream with me. When I didn't finish dinner, he'd say, "You can't have ice cream," but he relented—because that's what grandparents do.

I made friends with kids in the hospital because we were all there for so long. Some kids were in traction-type beds, which looked weird and scary to a little kid like me. They were suspended in mid-air inside this wheel-looking thing, and their heads were in a metal skullcap that had bolts screwed into the sides of their heads. Whenever I saw something like that, it just freaked me out. It made me wonder, *Am I next?*

All the time, I asked my mom, "Is that going to happen to me?"

I was in constant fear of the unknown in the hospital and what they were going to do next. Thankfully, I was spared from being put in halo-gravity traction, which generally helps stretch and straighten compressed or curved spines.

Walk This Way

After a couple of major surgeries on my legs, I was ready to learn how to walk independently with crutches. I still crawled a lot at home because I could move so much faster to keep up with my sisters when they ran around.

Around five years old, Nana started teaching me to walk. She built parallel bars out of old plumbing pipe left over after building her house. Nana had designed and constructed her own house. (More on that later.) The bars seemed long, but were a little over five feet, the length of Nana's fireplace hearth. She put the bars in front of the fireplace and drew outlines of feet with a black felt-tip pen on an old pink bed sheet.

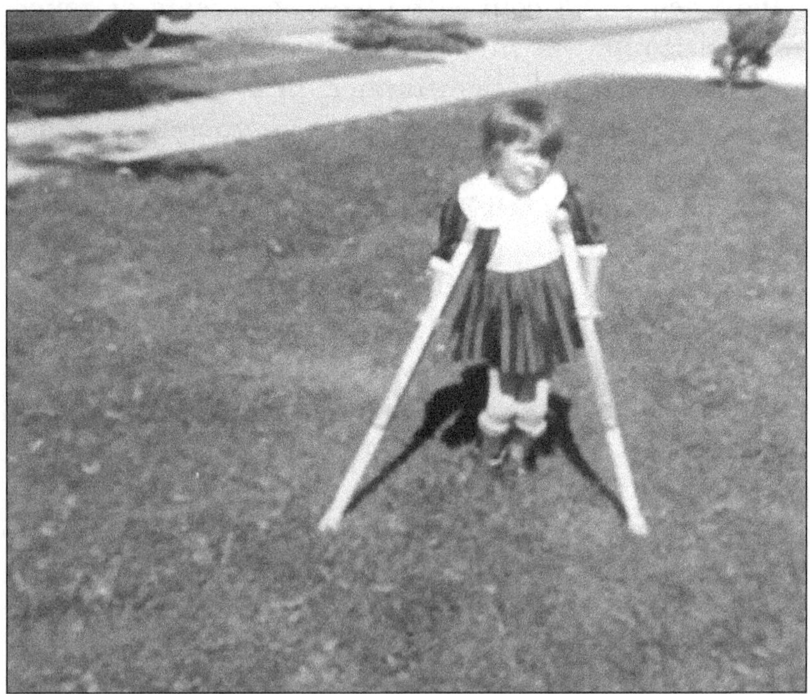

Teri walking independently, 1970.

Nana put me at one end of the bars, told me to hold on and match my feet to the footprints she had drawn on the sheet. The footprints were my guide for placing one foot in front of the other. When I first tried, I did it, no problem! When everyone got home that same day, Nana had me show them how I could walk. After that, I think Nana realized everything the doctors might say may not necessarily be true—especially the piece about "she won't ever amount to much."

Nana was stubborn and usually accomplished what she put her mind to. Obviously, she passed along some of that stubbornness, determination, and independence to me. These have served me well throughout my life. But as tough as Nana could be, she also had her soft side. Even after I learned to walk, if I told Nana I had to go the bathroom, she'd carry me. Mom would get mad at Nana and tell her, "Let Teri go to the bathroom by herself."

If Mom wasn't around, Nana still carried me, even when I was about seven years old. I'd say, "Mom will get mad." Nana reassured me, "It's okay, don't tell your mom. I won't carry you when you're older, but right now I know you really have to go, and I'm afraid you won't make it."

To this day, I love Nana for loving me so much.

Teri in front of her grandparents' house 1971.

Chapter 3
Don't Cry!

While learning to walk with leg braces, Nana encouraged me to push myself. If people made fun of me, she told me not to let them see me cry. Instead, Nana taught me to be strong and stand up for myself when someone bullied me. I learned to have some kind of smart comeback when people were mean. My sisters and friends also spent a lot of time defending me, verbally and physically.

Sticking Up for Me

In all the places we lived when I was young, there were always kids that made fun of me. Traci was the tomboy who beat up anybody that messed with me. One time in Eugene when I was about four, my twin was pulling me in a red wagon when some older boy called me a "retarded crippled freak."

I yelled back at him, "I'm not retarded," as though "crippled freak" was fine. I knew I just didn't want to be called retarded—because I wasn't! Traci's response was to give the kid a black eye. He ran home crying and told his mommy. She brought her kid to our apartment door and said to my mom, "Look what your daughter did to my son!"

Mom simply asked, "What did he say to my daughter?"

That was the end of that discussion.

My twin has been sticking up for me all her life. As adults, I've gotten more careful with what I tell Traci about things people say to me. She may not physically beat them up these days, but she verbally kicks their asses. When Traci gets mad, watch out, it's vicious.

Fighting Back

As I grew, I got better at maintaining a tough exterior, especially around mean people, and my family usually backed me up. A good example of my family's loyalty happened when I was in the sixth grade and one of the neighbor boys, Fred, was especially mean. Honestly, he was a little asshole, saying hurtful things to me whenever he could. One day, my friend Kelly and I were playing my air hockey game, outside, and Fred came by. He made some strange hand gesture, slapping his hand sideways and curling it up against his chest, calling me a "retard" in a garbled voice. I guess that was his version of what a "retard" might sound and look like. I glared at him and said, "Take a picture, it might last longer!" Kelly and I said that to anyone who stared at me—adults included.

That day, Kelly and Traci chased Fred, caught him, and dragged him over to me. They held him down and let me punch him in the face a few times. When I grabbed his hair to pull it, it was so greasy it grossed me out and I screamed. After that, we made fun of Fred's greasy hair. It was my way of fighting back and dishing out some pain of my own!

When we lived in Florida in the early 1970s, there was a strange incident that Traci reminded me of years later. It was one more example of my sister defending me when a bully harassed me. At our apartment there was a swimming pool with a cool slide. My sisters helped me get up to the top and I'd slide down. One day, a neighbor girl was swimming with us, and she watched my sisters help me get up the slide. She called me a "cripple" and Traci got so mad she went up to the girl, pulled her nose plug over her nose, and snapped it on her face. Then Traci said, "Don't ever call my sister that name!"

The neighbor ran home crying. Either Traci felt bad, or she was made to apologize (I believe it was the latter), so she went next door to apologize to the girl. Her mom answered the door and said, "Wait out here, she will be right out."

Traci sat down on the front steps and waited. A few minutes later, the girl's mom came out and poured water over Traci's head. Stunned, Traci went home and told our stepdad at that time, Ed, and his friend. They went next door to talk to the mean mom, but she wouldn't answer the door, so Ed grabbed all the clothes hanging on the clothesline and threw them in the mud. That was that!

Crying & Lonely

Mostly, I cried because I was lonely. I didn't just cry because I felt bad about something that was said to me. In truth, I cried because I wanted friends and people to see that I was "normal." I wanted to have friends who called me on the phone and asked me to play with them; when I got older, I wanted friends to hang out with on the weekends, or go on a date, or be included—the same things that most kids want.

I didn't always cry when people made fun of me. With time, I learned some good sarcastic comebacks based on whatever was said to me. And I'm quite comfortable making my point with some good swear words. What I lack in mobility, I have definitely compensated with verbal acuity punctuated with swearing. I have never been the quiet, sweet, invisible girl with the physical disability! You know when I'm in the room.

As a teenager, the mean comments got to me even more. Alone in my room at night, I cried. My family often said, "Don't feel sorry for yourself."

So, if I did cry, I tried to do it alone. Usually, I just thought, *Fuck them.*

Swearing in a Frustrating World

Perhaps because I learned to hide my tears so well, I ended up with lots of anger and early along, I learned how to swear, probably to defend myself. My favorite word in any grammatical variation is the word "fuck"; like, motherfucker, fucking asshole, or fucking moron. I've used it a lot lately to describe my intense dislike of some politicians.

Sometimes, I like to combine words, like idi-fucking-ot, which translates to "fucking idiot." But I also use swear words to convey many emotions—from happy to sad to pissed off. And I'll often top off with a big dose of sarcasm. People who use the word fuck and like it, they know what I'm talking about.

My family knows all too well my reputation for a colorful vocabulary. Most like it when I swear because they say it's not offensive—they think it's funny because they don't expect swear words to come out of my mouth. Most of the time, I don't think people listen to me, or they just think of me as a sweet, nice, little girl, no matter what I say or do. My swearing and sarcasm may also have something do with finding ways to express myself with force in an extremely frustrating world that wants to treat me as invisible. Psychological studies have found that swearing is a sign of greater language fluency and intelligence, not less. Based on their findings, I'm a fucking genius.

I started swearing when I was young; probably as soon as I started feeling the need to defend myself. My family wasn't always a fan of my swearing, but as an adult they now accept that swearing is a part of me and realize it's how I express myself—no matter the emotion. Now, they would think something was wrong with me if I quit swearing. I do not buy into the belief that if you swear, you must not have a large vocabulary. I have a large vocabulary, and I still swear!

Don't misunderstand. I was not free to swear as a kid. I did it when there wasn't adult supervision. And as an adult, I swear freely. My sister Traci warned me to be careful around her young children, Alix and Aaron, saying, "Don't swear in front of the kids."

At the time, I tried to refrain myself when visiting my young niece and nephew. However, one time when Traci was vacuuming, she hit a table and yelled, "Fuck!"

I turned and said with a giggle, "You're swearing!"

I know when to hold my tongue.

Traci (left), Teri, and Tami in matching Easter outfits, 1968.

Chapter 4
On the Move

Ages are sometimes a blur for me, but I think of parts of my life in terms of where I lived. We moved around so much that I grouped my experiences around where we were living at any given time.

We moved from Eugene to San Jose, California in fall 1970. While living in the Bay Area, I had another operation on my legs, this time at the San Francisco Shriners Hospital, which later relocated to Sacramento. After that operation to straighten my legs, I got my first set of quad canes—canes with four legs—that I called my crutches.

During this time, my mom married a musician, Ed Johnson, who had his own band, "Johnson and Johnson," so I call this my San Jose period. When the band was on the road, we sometimes traveled with them if we didn't have school.

Climbing a Tree

One of my San Jose memories was climbing a tree when I was about seven years old. Well, I didn't actually climb a tree, but I did a chin up on a lower branch. At the time, I told myself that I had climbed the tree because it was something I longed to do, but a photo shows me doing a chin up, using the seat of my walker, located in the grass under the tree. I had an old metal walker with a seat that I used outside so I could sit down when I wanted, or someone could push me fast and jump on the back.

Tree climbing never quite happened for me, although I longed for it. However, there was the time my sisters tied a rope around my torso and literally dragged me up a tree. After that, I decided I could say I really climbed a tree.

Living in Florida

After San Jose, we moved to Florida and lived in Coco Beach briefly, and then Satellite, Florida, following Ed's band. Sometimes, when the band was on the road and if we were lucky, we'd get to stay at a Holiday Inn because the band played the same venue for a few days. The band members were basically lounge lizards, mostly playing gigs like the Holiday Inn. Usually, we'd stay in motels with swimming pools, so the three of us swam a lot, and we regularly ate Snack Pack pudding out of the vending machines while the band rehearsed for hours. Funny what one remembers from a childhood.

We also swam at a nudist camp where Mom and Ed had a membership. We swam in the pool naked and played on the teeter-totters with other naked kids. During nudist camp visits, I was free of casts, so I played along. At that point, I was still young and far less self-conscious about my body and surgical scars, or other abnormalities that later turned into constant reminders as I grew.

When I think about it now, Ed and Mom were the epitome of 1970s hippies. At their outdoor wedding, Mom wore a yellow dress with a tiny, flower pattern and a crown of garland flowers on her head. My sisters and I were flower girls in long pink dresses. I had casts on my legs that stretched just below my knees, and my toenails were painted pink.

Bedtime with Teri in the middle, always.

Mom used to dress the three of us alike in clothes that she or Nana sewed. Often, we dressed up in our matching outfits and went to the Holiday Inn, or wherever the band played. Decked out in our matching outfits, we'd sit and eat dinner, and drink Shirley Temples during the band's sets. Sometimes, Ed invited the three of us on stage to sing "Candy Man" by Sammy Davis Jr. I barely whispered into the microphone, a bit frozen from stage fright. Still, everyone said, "Aww," and clapped.

In Florida, my sisters and I all slept together in a double bed, and I got stuck in the middle. Before falling off to sleep, I ended up being the judge for whatever activity Tami and Traci were competing at on any given night. As judge, I could never just be right because one of them would be disappointed, no matter what I decided. They liked lip-syncing, so I had to decide who was the best. I also had to judge who could jump on the pogo stick the longest. This meant I had to count every jump each of them made to determine the winner. When they got good, I was counting into the hundreds.

While traveling with the band during our school vacations, we got to know a young woman, Lynda Carter, who was a singer in the band along with Ed. Later, Lynda became a television celebrity in her role as Wonder Woman. At the time I knew Lynda, she was about 19 and lived with us for several months. I saw her as a very pretty woman with long brown hair parted in the middle. She wore long fake eyelashes that highlighted her sparkling blue eyes. Sometimes, Lynda wrote us letters when she traveled. I suppose you could call that a "brush with fame."

Odd Babysitters

During that unusual time in Florida, we had a succession of flipped out babysitters. One teenage girl stood at the kitchen table holding a bottle of Windex, threatening to spray our food if we didn't eat. Another one, probably in her early twenties, was often tripping on some hallucinogenic and at times rolled on the floor mumbling incoherently. One time, I sat on the floor next to her and watched her hallucinate, trying to figure out what was going on. The only thing I understood was her mumbling, "What about Teri?"

I responded, "What about me?"

Of course, that went nowhere. She just continued rolling around on the floor, babbling. We became her babysitter.

The worst babysitter was a girl who cared for us when Ed and Mom were out of town. Mom left the keys to her Renault, white with red vinyl interior. Mom told Tami the car was not to be driven, only in an emergency. Of course, once Mom left the babysitter decided to take us for a ride. When she loaded Traci and me in the backseat, Tami reminded the sitter about Mom's instructions: Do not drive the car unless there's an emergency.

The babysitter looked at Tami and said, "Fine. You can stay here."

Tami, not happy about being left alone, jumped in the car. The babysitter couldn't drive a stick, so the car lurched and stalled, lurched and stalled. Along the way, the babysitter decided to pick up a guy we kids thought was a hitchhiker—another brilliant move. The hitcher drove us all back to the house. The babysitter told us not to tell our mom she took the car out for a spin. Or she threatened, "I'll kill you."

The next morning, surprise! The car was gone. Mom and Ed got home and reported the car stolen. Tami came clean and told Mom about our adventure. Mom asked, "Why didn't you say anything?"

Tami blurted, "Because the babysitter said she would kill us!"

Later, Tami told me the hitchhiker was the babysitter's boyfriend. I don't know where my mom found these babysitters, but it made for an interesting visit. It wasn't until years later that I realized how odd our babysitters were. As a kid, I thought it was no big deal because it just seemed like the way things were. My sense of normal was weird. Now, I think, *Wow if that happened today, it might be on an episode of* Cops.

I'm sure many people reading this might think I had an out-of-control childhood, but I think it was within the realm of normal for that time. It was the '70s, man!

Tami, Teri, and Traci playing dress up, 1971.

Chapter 5

Back to Oregon

My mom's marriage to Ed broke up after about a year because Ed was cheating on her. It seems Mom had a knack for picking guys she thought were exciting, but in the end, they didn't treat her well.

In the early 1970s, Mom and the three of us landed back in Sandy, Oregon, living with our grandparents, Nana and Bapa, for several months. They lived in Sandy, a small community nestled in a beautiful, forested area. Their house was at the 34-mile marker off Highway 26 on the way to majestic Mt. Hood, a dormant volcano with snow-covered slopes that provided skiing almost year around. In the winter, I could smell the smoke from their fireplace puffing out of the chimney as we drove up the long, black-topped driveway toward their cozy house.

I loved living with my grandparents because their house felt like home, and we usually had a lot of fun. We attended Welches Elementary School, not far from Mt. Hood, which was a good experience. I had friends, including little boys I liked, and a nice teacher who thought I was smart, and she let me help the other kids with math. In her class, I felt like I was a part of a group—not separate from.

Mom's younger sister, our Aunt Carol, or as we liked to call her, Auntie, had two sons, Jeff and Rodney. We played with our cousins a lot, and Mom and Auntie helped one another with childcare. When the five grandchildren were at Nana and Bapa's, we played nonstop; built forts, shot BB guns, and rode skateboards down the driveway sitting on our butts, crashing into the grass before the end of the driveway.

My sisters and cousins tried to make me a part of everything. Most of the time, my grandparents treated me like the other grandkids, except for certain things—like giving me a five-minute head start on the Easter egg hunt, or when we all played baseball on our knees and crawled around the bases in the backyard so I could be included.

Expected to Be Independent

One of the things I love most about my family is that they all treated me normally, which led to my becoming a very independent adult. But the two people who influenced me the most were my maternal grandparents, Nana and Bapa. My independent grandmother was my greatest influence, especially in my early years. Nana was a great role model. Almost a decade before I was born, Nana had built her own house from the foundation up.

The house was on 125th street off Division in Southeast Portland and in those days that was considered countryside. Nana was a married woman when she inherited land from her stepdad after his death. She wanted to build a house and reasoned that if she could read a sewing pattern, then she should be able to read blueprints for a house. So, Nana went to Portland's city hall, looked at plans, found one she liked, and proceeded to build a three-bedroom, two-bath, ranch-style house with a double-car garage.

Nana and Bapa—Millie and Robert Goldsmith—on their wedding day, 1943.

Whenever Bapa got his paycheck and the bills were paid, he'd give Nana whatever was left so she could buy more building materials. When we were younger, Nana told us great stories about building her house and I loved hearing these stories, repeatedly, because Nana was so proud of her work. She was a great inspiration to me.

One of my favorite stories is about the time Nana was pouring the foundation for the house and Bapa slipped and fell into the wet cement. She laughed so hard she almost wet her pants. Nana quickly helped Bapa get up and out of the cement, worried he'd be stuck. She hosed him off before the cement dried, most likely laughing the whole time. Years later, whenever Nana told this story, she still laughed hardily—maybe even harder than when it happened!

Nana's house had lots of special touches that she added for convenience and mid-century aesthetics. Every ceiling had a different texture on it. The living room ceiling had small twirls throughout, a pattern Nana created by twisting her wrist back and forth with a small whisk broom until the entire ceiling was covered. Her wrist was sore from the repetitive motion, but she was pleased because the ceiling looked great. Under the house, Nana added more footings than were required for extra stability and she made the crawl space bigger than required for easier access.

The whole house was modern when Nana built it in 1958. She even installed an intercom with a radio and played music in all the rooms, often. She liked to sing along, belting out the lyrics. The intercom also helped avoid door-to-door salesmen. She'd answer the door via the intercom to say she wasn't interested in what they were selling. Or Nana would say, "My husband will be home soon."

With 20/20 hindsight, I really do believe most of my successes happened because Nana believed in my potential from the day I was born, plus I had a family that treated me normally.

Sweet & Wild Times

Eventually, Mom got us an apartment in Portland at the Woodland Park Apartments, a place my sisters and I refer to as "Apartment 57" when talking about those times. When we lived in Apartment 57, I crawled around the house quite a bit as my most common mode of movement. It was fast and easy. At the same time, I also discovered I could walk all by myself if I put on my mom's ski boots. Those boots probably worked because they were so rigid and had lots of support. I'd put them on and clomp around, feeling great to almost be "normal."

Most weekends and during the summer, my sisters, cousins, and I spent a lot of time together at Nana and Bapa's house. We five got very close and found mischievous things to do together. Our grandparents' expansive backyard was ideal for playing baseball with a Wiffle Ball and bat. Nana put down knitted hot plate squares that we used as bases. If I was playing, Nana came up with the rule that we all had to play on our knees and crawl around the bases—just to even the playing field. It was fun playing baseball on our knees and the kids got into it. Jeff, who played baseball all through school, would get on his knees and whack the ball as hard as he could. It would go flying a long way into the neighbor's yard. Jeff made his little brother, Rodney, get the ball. Rodney was the youngest among us and got the most picked on, besides me. I was easy pickings!

During this time, Nana was also taking care of Grandma Great, her mother, who had dementia, a condition we simply called "senile" in the old days. Our great grandmother lived with Nana and Bapa until she died in 1981 at 91 years old. My grandparents had married in 1943, and they never lived alone until after Grandma Great's death, almost 40 years later. Bapa teasingly said he couldn't wait to chase his wife around the house naked! I hope he did.

When we visited, Nana let us help her make Bapa's lunch for the next day. Poor guy never got a full sandwich because she'd take a bite out of one half of his sandwich every night when she packed his lunch. Of course, when we helped, we did the same. Sometimes, Nana put a little love note in Bapa's lunch box or inside the actual sandwich, so he'd take a bite and out slid a note.

Nana and Bapa were quite a love story. Everyone should have a story like theirs. I wanted a story like theirs! Bapa finally retired in 1979 and spent lots of

Hanging out at Nana and Bapa's house, 1971.

time with his wife. They were so happy living near Mt. Hood, a great place to grow old together, and for us to grow up. The five grandkids have great memories of our times with our grandparents. To this day, when we are all together, we end up reminiscing about those sweet and wild times.

Old Enough to Tease

When we got a little older, around 10, my sisters started picking on me, but it was mostly in a loving way. They hid around a corner in the house and grabbed me as I was coming down the hallway. Tami sat on my stomach while Traci held my arms down. They tickled me and while I was laughing, Tami would try spitting in my mouth, sucking the loogie back into her mouth right before it hit me. Sometimes, the spit hit my face or got in my mouth. I was laughing from the tickling, screaming with disgust, and ultimately, enduring the torture.

Tami and Traci also pinned me down, bit the ends off Red Vines licorice sticks and blew air up my nose through the licorice. Nana inevitably came and saved me. I'm sure the high-pitched screaming of young girls drove her crazy. As fair play, Nana would get down on the floor and hold Tami or Traci in a scissor lock and squeeze them until they said, "Uncle."

They laughed and said, "Uncle, uncle!" Once they gave up, Nana would say, "Leave Teri alone." Then she'd go back into the kitchen.

One time at my aunt's house, Tami, Traci, Jeff and Rodney were running around the back field behind the house, filling up a white plastic bucket with garter snakes. I was minding my own business, sitting on the front porch in a lawn chair. Suddenly, all four of them ran up on the porch and excitedly yelled, "Look Teri!" The bucket was filled almost to the top with wriggling snakes. A split second later, they dumped the bucket of snakes on my lap and ran off the porch laughing! I screamed bloody murder, stood up, and grabbed the front porch railing, probably faster than anyone had ever seen me move!

Aunt Carol came running from inside the house, opened the screen door and saw all the snakes slither through the weave on the lawn chair, onto the ground. At the time, that scared the shit out of me. I was pissed off and cried! If I could've run after them, I would have beaten the crap out of them! If someone other than my sisters and cousins had done that to me, the four of them would have beaten the crap out of the culprits. My family could pick on me, but nobody else could. The lasting scar from that prank is that I still hate snakes, and I am afraid of them.

Chapter 6

New Schools and Finding Friends

By age 10, I had gone to so many schools I stopped remembering most of their names. They all became a blur since I rarely stayed at a school for more than one consecutive year. The exception was the Holladay Center for Crippled Children in Portland, which I attended for two years when we lived in Apartment 57. My time at that school was equivalent to the fifth and sixth grades.

During this time, I started having knee problems. I couldn't lock my knees, so walking became even more difficult. I got tired quickly and it wore down my knees. I switched to a walker around sixth grade and then I was able to put more weight on the walker.

The Cool Crippled Kid

There were some nice kids at Holladay Center, and I made good friends, especially with Lisa. We had sleepovers and spent a lot of time hanging out together. The two of us did not have severe handicaps and we both had the same feelings about how we saw ourselves compared to most of the other kids with disabilities.

Most of the kids at Holladay Center dealt with severe physical handicaps, so we all had to wear ugly, black, leather padded helmets in case we fell. The floors in the school were made of hard rubber to help deter injuries for those who fell frequently. Most of the kids were limited in their physical activities and many of them drooled a lot, leaving their chins and the fronts of their shirts wet.

Of course, I didn't think I fit in at Holladay Center. I thought of myself as different from them. Instead, I thought of myself as the cool, crippled one. The truth is, I did not want to be like them or let myself act like them. Lisa felt similarly, which bonded us even further.

When families visited the school for events, all the "regular" kids in the families dressed in the latest fashions, but the "crippled" kids attending Holladay Center wore things like plaid pants and other fashion-challenged clothes, especially for the hip 1970s. Added to the fashion challenge was the sense that anyone at Holladay Center who wore glasses had tape on the frames. I didn't wear glasses, so I was even more aware of this.

Most of us wore leg braces, which made any hip fashion statement even more difficult. I often thought, *You'd think the parents might help their children out in the wardrobe department—anything to make them less of an eyesore to other kids.*

Fortunately, Mom or my sisters didn't let me leave the house dressed badly, so I'm sure this fed my sense of being cool and different. I can't help but think that feeling contributed to my shopping addiction. I love shoes, clothes, and makeup, acutely aware of how I look and how people might think of me.

A Special Friend

I had a special friend at Holladay; someone I think about to this day. Tim had blondish hair, fair skin with freckles, and blue eyes. He also had Muscular Dystrophy (MD). Tim's wheelchair was light blue, and his legs stretched straight out on the footrests in front of him. He was very weak, but he had to push his manual wheelchair with all his might, and it only moved a few inches with each push. I felt badly for Tim, so I walked next to him on my quad canes and pulled his footrest. This was my small way to give him an extra shove. The teachers told me, "Let Tim push himself. This is exercise for him."

Since MD isn't curable and the progression of the disease can't be stopped, I never understood the teachers' thinking about Tim pushing himself. No matter how hard he tried, Tim's muscles weren't going to get stronger, only weaker. So, I secretly helped him when we were together. We became good friends and looked forward to seeing one another. Sometimes, we'd hide behind the gray concrete pillars at school, and he would give me a little kiss and we giggled. He'd call my house, impersonating Dracula, and say, "I want to suck your blood!"

After summer vacation, I returned to Holladay, looking forward to seeing Tim again. When I didn't see him at school, I asked a teacher where he was. "Oh, Tim died over the summer," the teacher told me matter-of-factly. Shocked, I walked around for weeks wondering, *How come I didn't know?*

Decades later I still wonder why that teacher said it so nonchalantly but didn't ask how I was doing with this news or how I felt. Whenever I think about Tim, it still bothers me that the teacher was so cold. No hug to comfort me, no sitting me down and explaining Tim's death and how some kids with MD can die young. Some things you never forget; for me, it's Tim's death and how I was told.

After I left Holladay Center, I lost touch with my friend Lisa, but years later we ran into each other at a Portland mall and ever since, we have remained friends.

Summer Camp Crush

For a couple of summers, I attended special camps for kids with disabilities. When I was about 11 years old, I went to Camp Easter Seals in Coos Bay, Oregon. It was a beautiful place located on North Lake of Tenmile Lake, along the Oregon coast. At that time, it was one of the few summer camps in the United States designed for what they labeled "crippled children."

When Camp Easter Seals first opened in the mid-1950s, it was a cutting-edge camp specifically designed for people with physical disabilities. There were ramps instead of stairs, an extra-wide recreation building for kids in wheelchairs, and lots of fun things for kids like me to do. The camp had comfy cabins with twin beds and showers. We ate our meals in a big lodge and engaged in camp activities in another large lodge. Fat healthy deer walked right up to campers on the lawn, and we'd feed them pancakes leftover from breakfast. On the lakeshore, there were docks where we fished, and speedboats for cruising the brilliant mountain lake.

The camp counselors were in their late teens to early twenties, which set me up for having one of my biggest crushes on a camp counselor. As it turned out, I spent much of my childhood having one-sided, major crushes. This counselor, Jim, wore red shorts and no shirt, and had tanned abs, olive skin, white teeth, and loose, thick, curly brown hair. During my week at camp, Jim often sat with me on the dock, and we fished. I thought he was cool because he speared fish. One day I was reeling in lots of trout with help from Jim and ended up catching more fish than any other camper. My fishing talents were announced at dinner that night and you could say I was one happy camper.

I loved when Jim physically picked me up and carried me. At night, Jim came into my cabin and gave me a little kiss goodnight on the cheek or lips. He smelled like Brut Cologne, a scent I connect with memories of Jim to this day. One night, Jim climbed through my window to say goodnight. Don't worry, he wasn't a pervert, nothing more ever happened. I'm sure he knew I had a crush on him, so he played along, being so sweet and giving me extra attention.

One summer after I got back from camp, Jim called me at home. He just wanted to say hello. I was so happy. I had a photo of us at camp and on the back of the photo he had written "Jim + Teri" with a red heart around our names. I lost that photo somewhere along the way of frequent moves and life happenings, but I still remember it so clearly. In the photo, we are sitting on the grass, me on his lap, wearing Levis, a red hoodie, and my favorite shoes—brown suede waffle stompers. I had long brown hair and a deep tan. We both had huge grins, and I wonder if he had just tried to tickle me or something. We had become friends during my time at camp, and this camp crush boosted my self-confidence as a pre-teen.

Regular School

Tami and Traci went to "regular" public school. This bothered me because there were times I went to the same school as my sisters, and at other times, I had to go to a "special school." When I was not at the same school, I felt as if I was missing something. To this day, I still feel that way; if people are doing something that I can't do, I'm missing out. It sounds immature, I know, but I feel like that because there were many things while growing up where I felt excluded because of my CP. That's why, as an adult, I now do things that people assume I can't do— or wouldn't do—because I have CP.

With the passage of the Individuals with Disabilities Education Act in 1973, mainstreaming crippled kids into the public schools was the big thing. Eventually, the educational system stopped seeing us as "crippled kids" and started referring to us as "children with disabilities," or "handicapped," and eventually, "students with special needs." I thought just saying kids or students without a qualifier would have been great.

After two years at Holladay Center, I was mainstreamed into a regular public school in Portland called Sacramento Elementary School. The only problem was I had to repeat the sixth grade because school administrators thought I might be slower since I had gone to Holladay Center. My older sister, Tami, was in the eighth grade, and Traci, my twin, had moved up to the seventh grade at Heights Junior High School. Once again, I got the message that somehow my physical challenges made me mentally slower. That was the common stereotype of people with physical disabilities in the 1970s, a stereotype that persists to this day. So once again, I was stuck. Not until high school was I once again at the same school with my sisters.

A Lifelong Friend

One good thing about repeating the sixth grade was meeting Kelly, who became my friend, and some 40 years later continues to be my best friend. Kelly was a year younger, and she was also the youngest sister of Tami's friend, Michelle. So, I knew Kelly before attending Sacramento, but we cemented our friendship at Sacramento Elementary. I was impressed that Kelly, who was considered normal—no physical disabilities—wanted to hang out with me. At school, Kelly introduced me to her friends without ever referring to my CP and I felt like I fit in with the rest of the kids.

At recess, my new friends let me play Red Rover. They also let me play catch with a football, sitting in a chair.

Someone came over and tackled me, and I fell off the chair, which was great fun! Unfortunately, the teachers saw our football game and put a stop to all my physical games at recess, treating me differently, and once again setting me apart from the other kids. My thoughts about those teachers were basically, *Fuckers! As soon as someone treats me normal, you have to ruin it!*

Still, Kelly and I figured out ways to be physically active and play games. We got good at playing handball—to the point where we competed against other people. She pushed me in my wheelchair and I hit the ball against the wall. I had fun doing all the things I wasn't supposed to do—or at least, what people thought I shouldn't do.

My happiness at Sacramento Elementary didn't last long. For the first time, Mom was able to afford renting a house, so we had to move again, and our new home was out of the school district. Kelly and I talked on the phone, and once I moved to another part of Portland, we took to writing long letters; some were 30 pages long.

My new grammar school was, as usual, filled with all new kids and new teachers, and more questions, and more stupid comments. The first day at the new school, my teacher introduced me just by name without any additional information about me. He said I'd be at that school the remainder of the school year. The questions were left to the kids to ask. Once again, I got all the typical questions and comments.

"What's wrong with you?"

"What's cerebral palsy?"

"Why do you have scars on your legs?"

My time at that school was brief because everything was about to change, again.

Teri and her dad, Brian, riding their horse Valentine at their new home in Tucson, about 1977.

Chapter 7
A New Dad and a New Home

A major event changed the direction of our family when we were living in Apartment 57 in Portland—we met our biological dad for the first time. He came to Portland for a visit and called my grandparents to ask for our phone number. We didn't know him. The only image we had of our dad was a grainy picture on his business card made of heavy, orange cardstock.

Stranger at Our Door

From our apartment window I watched a man walk toward our front door. I asked Mom, "Who's that guy? He's cute."

The stranger was six feet tall, had the slender physique of an athlete, and brown wavy hair. "That's your dad," she replied matter-of-factly.

Shocked, I tried to play it cool, act nonchalant, but anxiously wondering what his visit meant. It really didn't register that this was my dad. He knocked on the door and Mom called Tami and Traci in from outside.

We all stood in the living room staring at this man named Brian. As Mom introduced us one by one, I thought, *He must already know who we are!*

Growing up, people said I looked a lot like my dad—and when I looked at him for the first time that day, I saw what they meant. We both have dark hair with a widow's peak, dark eyes, and the same jawline and nose. His mom, my Grandma Trudy, looked similar as well. She was petite and so am I.

At first, there was lots of nervous small talk among all of us, but before long, we grew more comfortable with the idea of having our dad in the room. Brian stayed in Portland a couple days, getting to know us. He carried me around a lot when we were out and about, the scent of his aftershave embedded in my memory. One day, he took us to a pet store and bought us a bird, which made us like him even more. As our dad drove us to different places, I sat in the front passenger seat of his car, answering his questions about Mom, my sisters, and me. Brian was trying to get an idea of our day-to-day life, who we were, and what was going on for us.

I soon learned my dad had the gift of gab, which is probably where I get mine. He had been a successful general manager of car dealerships, probably in large part because of his skills as a conversationalist. I also learned that his athleticism was the result of his high school years as a champion pole vaulter at David Douglas High School.

Years later, my dad shared that when he first got to know me, he thought I was well spoken for a young girl, and I had a good head on my shoulders. We still have long conversations about the family, and he wants to know what I think.

After going to bed at night, I could hear my parents talking in whispered tones in the living room. I couldn't tell what they were talking about, but it seemed important. A few days later, when our dad told us goodbye, I cried because I wondered if I would see him again.

That first visit ended up being the start of my parents' second attempt at marriage. It also determined our eventual move from Portland to Tucson, Arizona

Moving to Tucson

Within a couple months after meeting my dad, my parents got back together, and we all moved to Tucson. We lived in a big house with a swimming pool, walk-in closets, and stables with horses. Our dad's house was so different than anything we had lived in before. We were used to living in apartments or small houses, sharing beds, rooms, and bathrooms. This house was about the size of three or four apartments combined. Traci and I shared a huge room with two, separate walk-in closets that were big enough for a small table, chair, and my big pink, furry, foot-shaped rug. I spent lots of time in that comfy closet, finding my own private space, writing in my diary. I pasted pictures of Freddy Prinze inside my diary—he was my big crush. In 1977, when Prinze shot himself in the head, I cried my eyes out in the safety of my closet hideaway.

I had mixed feelings about our new home and my dad. It took some time to adjust to this new life with another person in our family. I was sad to leave Portland and my friend Kelly. At the time, I didn't even know there was a place called Tucson, or where it was. But my dad said he'd get me a Shetland pony, so, I said, "Ok!"

What did I know? Besides, it's not like I could've stayed in Portland even if I had wanted to. We were moving to Arizona no matter what. When Tami got the news about our move, she locked herself in the bathroom in protest and said she wasn't going. We went anyway.

Getting Used to a Dad

Having a dad in our lives took some getting used to. I was the last of us siblings to call this man Dad. I asked things like, "When is he coming home from work?" Or I'd call him Brian, but not Dad. It felt weird because I wasn't used to having a dad, except for Ed, briefly, and he was now out of our lives. It was my grandpa that filled that role. Bapa was the best Dad I knew!

Brian bribed me with candy or something I wanted to get me to call him Dad. On the weekends, Mom had him take me on drives to get soft-serve ice cream at Dairy Queen. We talked while I ate my chocolate ice cream; I liked that. After a few months, I started calling him Dad.

At Last, My Pony!

Over time, my dad seemed to ask my opinions regularly about events and people. If something was going on in the family, he'd ask what I thought. I'd tell him about our friends or my thoughts on his latest idea to move somewhere. I think he looked at me like the family librarian—I had information about everyone. To this day, when we talk about family matters, he often says, "You are right, I totally agree." However, there is one big exception; we do not agree on politics!

My dad did keep his promise, he got me a pony, except it was a mean black-and-white Shetland pony named Patrick. He bucked me off once, but I didn't let go of the reigns. Just like in the movies, Patrick dragged me behind him until I finally let go. After that, I didn't ride him unless he was in his corral. One time, I sent my friend Kelly some of Patrick's tail hair. I just wanted her to see and feel it; I was sharing a piece of my life in Arizona with Kelly in Oregon.

We also had a 19-year-old Appaloosa named Valentine. He was a good old horse, and I used to ride him with Tami or Traci in Tucson's dry washes. One time, Traci and I fell off and I ended up with a concussion. Another time, Tami and I were riding Valentine in a full gallop when my nose slammed into Tami's back and I got a bloody nose. Obviously, horses and I did not mix, but I loved moving fast, which has influenced me to seek out anything that gets my adrenaline going.

Tami and Traci had to shovel horseshit, keep the corrals clean, and feed and water our four horses. If Tami forgot her chores during the day, she had me go with her at night because she was afraid. While she cleaned the stalls, I sat on Valentine, fully aware that I would not be of much help fighting off some kind of scary attacker.

More New Schools

The third school I attended during the sixth grade—which should've been the seventh grade—was Tanque Verde Elementary School in Tucson. This move was a turning point in my life. Out of all the places I lived, Tucson turned out to be the place where I was treated the most like a regular girl. I even had friends! At times, I might have been almost popular. However, it didn't start out that way or end up that way.

At Tanque Verde, I had a couple friends who did things with me. My friend Kathy had a twin brother, Tommy, who had mild handicaps with CP. It was barely noticeable, except that he walked on his tiptoes. Tommy's mom always yelled from the car window when she dropped him off at tennis practice, "Heel down, Tommy, heel down."

I had a major crush on Tommy for years because he was a nice guy and cute. I liked spending the night at Kathy's house so I could stare at Tommy. He didn't like me like that, so I had to settle to just like him from afar.

In seventh grade, I went to Emily Gray Junior High in Tucson and finally, my sisters and I all attended the same school. The administration still placed me a year behind my twin, academically, but at least we were at the same school.

A girl I had met in the sixth grade, Cindy, became one of my best friends in the seventh grade. In fact, I'm still friends with her some 40 years later. Cindy was beautiful and smart and got straight A's. She'd let me copy her science papers and in turn, I taught her some street smarts, especially with our science teacher whom I considered a real creep. This teacher had brown, greasy hair that he parted to one side, and his beard was scruffy. He wore short-sleeved, buttoned-down shirts, and sandals with socks. One Saturday, Cindy and I were hanging out at the school, just messing around. Cindy was pushing me in my chair and accidentally ran me into a wall. She freaked out, but I was laughing the whole time, screaming some variation of, "Fuck, we are going to crash!" It wasn't the first time that had happened. We were laughing about the crash, thinking no one else was around. Suddenly, the science teacher opened the door from his classroom and called to us across the yard to join him for, of all things, lemon cream pie. Cindy, sweet and naïve, thought that sounded good and was about to say, "Ok!"

Without a moment's hesitation, I quietly said to Cindy, "We are not going in there! He gives me the creeps!" Then I yelled to the teacher, "No thanks!"

Fast forward years later, Cindy called to tell me, "My dad heard on the news that Mr. Creep was arrested for child molestation!"

I was not surprised by the news. "I told you he was fucked up! That explains the cot in the back room of his classroom!"

A Townhouse in Tucson

By the end of the seventh grade, my life changed once again. My parents sold the house and horses, and we all moved to a nearby townhouse. And not long after, the day came when my sisters started getting interested in boys. My dad's reasoning for the move was, "We sold the house and horses because the girls are interested in boys."

His explanation wasn't too convincing since I first noticed cute boys when I was in kindergarten! I think he just wanted to move closer to town. The boys did start knocking on the townhouse door more frequently in junior high and high school, perhaps in part because we were closer to town. Tami's first boyfriend was Darin, a middle school classmate. I saw them kissing once on the front patio and I was very interested to learn more. We talked about boys a lot in middle school and listened to the stereo in Tami's room. To this day, when I hear anything from the Rolling Stones' album, *Some Girls,* I see myself in Tami's room, laying on the floor, reading the album sleeve. Good times.

Traci had boys knocking on the door, too, but she didn't have a steady boyfriend in high school. Over time, I developed friendships with some of the guys that hung around our house. They were nice to me, but they were interested in my sisters for dating.

Eighth grade was back to hell. My mom signed me up to attend still another school, Townsend Middle School, which was a regular school but had one room where all the "special kids" were kept. Every couple of class periods I was allowed to join the "normal kids" for a math or English class. That was the school's idea of mainstreaming. My mom thought it would be good for me because someone told her it would be good for me; the reason I usually went to different schools than my sisters. This school had special classes like P.E. for kids with handicaps, which was supposed to be a good idea. I think it just slowed me down. I felt more introverted than usual, and I didn't make new friends.

Cindy stayed at Emily Grey Junior High, but somehow, we figured out how to remain friends. There was no such thing as social media in those days. We stayed at each other's houses when we could and figured out how to hang out with one another even when we attended different schools.

Despite the public-school system's efforts to mainstream students with physical disabilities, we were still set apart and treated differently. This was especially difficult and painful because I wanted to be treated the same. I think the normal students thought I was weird because they walked past that "special room" at Townsend and saw me in there with kids who had severe physical handicaps. Even the teacher in the special room once said, "I don't understand why you're here."

She let me help her with some of the students in the class, which made me feel a bit better about myself. But outside of that, I remember nothing else about that school except that I was lonely. When it was over, I was glad to leave and hoped for better experiences in high school.

Chapter 8
One More Surgery

After we had been in Tucson a few years, I had my last operation. In summer 1979, I had graduated from middle school, and I was ready to start high school. In September, I turned 15 and the plan was to get through the surgery and recover before starting high school.

Gaining Leg Flexibility

This operation straightened out my knees so I could straighten or "lock" them when standing. My knees couldn't do that before the operation, which made walking very tiring, and my knees hurt all the time. When I checked into the hospital at the University of Arizona, the doctors told me the cast would only go to the top of my thighs.

During surgery, the doctors decided to stretch out my hip muscles and the adductor muscles that allowed my legs to spread. When I woke up in the recovery room and tried to sit up, I couldn't. I looked under the sheet and saw that the cast went from the tips of my toes up to my chest with a plaster bar between my ankles that kept my legs apart. There was a hole in the front of the cast and a hole in back for going to the bathroom in a bedpan—and that was it.

Waking up to a full body cast was a terrible shock. It is the most vivid memory I have of an operation since it was so extreme, but also because most of my surgeries happened when I was still young.

While in the body cast, I could not move. My head, shoulders, and arms were the only exposed parts, besides my toes peeking out. I was at the mercy of everyone for everything, including my bathroom needs. For about a week I stayed at the hospital, trying to adjust to this new life with a full body cast.

Nurse Ratched

The nursing staff at the hospital was super nice to me. I was on morphine for pain, and a nurse came in every hour or two to turn my body in a different position. If I was uncomfortable, I could ring a call button to get more pain meds, and it usually was no problem.

One night, a different nurse I didn't know was on duty. When I rang the bell, she came to help me, but when I asked for a shot for pain, she said, "No." As this nurse proceeded to turn me, she said, "You're calling too much." While she scolded me, she roughly grabbed the bar between my legs with one hand, and my torso with her other hand. I literally almost bounced as she turned me.

When she was done, I asked her again for a shot to ease the pain, and she snapped back, "You don't need one."

Then, she moved my bed just far enough away from the nightstand where the phone sat. It was a sleepless night as I cried and tried to turn myself, holding on to the bed sidebars. It helped a little, but not much. My muscles were aching and sore, and my legs started cramping up from being in the same position for too long. I had visions of ripping off my cast. Afraid of Nurse Ratched's anger, I didn't call out for help; I just suffered through the night. longing to curl up and go to sleep.

Teri with her mom, after last surgery, 1979.

The next morning when my parents came to visit, I was crying. When they asked what happened, I told them. They said, "You should've called us!"

"I couldn't reach the phone!" I explained.

My parents went to the nurses' station and raised hell.

Home

Shortly after that incident, I went home. My sisters took turns sleeping in my room so they could turn me or help me if I had to go to the bathroom. The first night that Traci slept in my room there was one big problem: she sleeps like the dead. I needed to be turned, but I couldn't wake her up. I kept calling out, "Traci, Traci, Traci!"

Nothing. So, I started yelling, "Mom, Mom, Mom!" like Stewie from *Family Guy.* Mom finally came downstairs, angry because Traci didn't wake up. She got grounded and I felt guilty.

Once a week, I went back to the hospital and had the legs of the cast opened. Each time, the doctor straightened my legs a little more. It was excruciating and I got morphine to curb the pain. Once, I hallucinated about a bird flying through the room and everyone laughed when I told them what I was seeing. After the doctors placed little wedges behind my knees, they re-plastered the cast.

Everything I ate, I threw up. One time I even threw up on the cast man's feet. The doctors made a hole in the cast on my belly area to alleviate the nauseousness, but it didn't help. This miserable weekly routine continued until the cast finally came off a month later. There were 101 stitches in my legs—and they had to be pulled out, one by one. My cousin Jeff took photographs, documenting the torture I endured.

The first thing I did when I got home, cast free, was soak in a hot bath. It felt so good. As I soaked my skinny scaly legs, my skin yellow and peeling, I thought, *I'm shedding like a snake.*

On top of everything else, I had lost weight during my time in the body cast. I was almost 15 years old and weighed maybe 70 pounds. After that first bath, I felt free of the body cast. Finally! I was so hungry and ready to eat. Jeff and I ate burritos, and no puking!

Trade-Offs

With that final surgery, I had to pick what I'd rather have: straight legs, enabling me to walk further distances without tiring, or keep my bent legs with painful knees that allowed me to get up and down from the floor. I resigned myself to my new reality: *Can't have it all,* I told myself.

The surgeons had cut the muscle behind each of my knees, which resulted in my legs being much weaker. The great thing about this surgery was I could finally straighten my legs and lock my knees. The downside of the surgery was I couldn't bend my legs. No more crawling or getting up off the floor. To this day, some 40 years later, I still can't get up off the floor by myself because my legs don't bend.

That's the challenge for people with CP who have surgeries. It fixes one thing, but sometimes it prevents you from being able to do something you used to do. My knees can bend, but just not much, unless I bend them manually. My calves don't touch the back of my thighs.

Just Deal

After the surgery, I worried about being able to walk the same. I had to learn how to walk all over again, just as I was getting ready to start high school. My muscles were so weak after being in the cast for a month that when I first stood with support from my walker, my legs gave out. For at least a month, I was in my wheelchair full time. Three times a week I went to therapy to build up my leg strength to be strong enough to use my walker by the first day of high school.

During the first session with my physical therapist, Phil, he bent one of my legs for the first time since the cast had been removed. I screamed and cried from the severe pain. Rarely did I do that. As Phil slowly bent my leg, it felt as if he was breaking it. I had considered myself tough when it came to physical pain, but this pushed me close to my limits. On the other hand, throughout my life I have caved much faster with my emotional pain. Honestly, I'd much rather endure physical pain!

I hated exercising in front of people—it was so embarrassing. Again, I had no choice, so I did it. Early on in life I learned to just deal with things because I had no choice. Acceptance was my big lesson. I did not want to be a complainer, so I just had to go with the program and accept what was going on.

The good news is that I always had family around me. My sisters talked to me or entertained me when I was incredibly bored. When I was in a cast, they'd draw pictures all over it, somehow making an awful situation bearable. During the body cast period, they'd load me into a reclining wheelchair and take me to the pool in our townhouse complex where I watched them swim. We'd smoke a joint and I literally felt no pain.

One time when I was in the body cast, Traci and I smoked a joint while sitting on my bed and we accidentally burned a hole in the sheets. We were paranoid Mom would find it. Traci rolled me back and forth on the bed and got the old sheets off, put them in the washing machine, and put on new ones. We told Mom I had an accident on the sheets; we were good at coming up with believable excuses—or so we thought.

No matter what was going on, my family found a way to include me as best they could. They didn't act like I was a pain in the ass, even if I was. My whole family, cousins, aunts and uncles included, made me feel wanted and loved.

Of course, I also had to learn to swallow a lot of my feelings and not complain too much. If I complained, Mom said, "Stop feeling sorry for yourself."

This tough approach did make me stronger, for sure, but the truth is, I felt vulnerable so much of the time. To this day, I'm careful not to complain too much about anything.

Chapter 9
High School

When I began high school, I begged my mom and dad to let me go to Sabino High School with Tami and Traci. The principal of the school—someone I considered another dick in a long line of dicks—told them, "I don't advise it. Teri won't have any friends at Sabino."

I guess the principal thought no "normal kids" would want to be friends with a "crippled kid" like me. At that time, there were many misinformed decisions made on behalf of people with physical disabilities—decisions that were more harmful in the long run. It's as if I couldn't think for myself and the authority figures determined that they knew what was best. When I listened to him talk about me, I thought, *How would you know, fucker? You are dead wrong!*

In response to the principal's decision, my parents talked with me, listened, and decided I knew best. They threatened to sue the high school. So, that is how I got into Sabino High School in 1979 when most kids with physical handicaps were still sent to separate special schools. Or they were placed in regular public schools but in separate rooms, like zoo animals, in my opinion.

Just Treat Me Like a Normal Kid

The misery of lots of tutoring and extra classes paid off after my freshman year at Sabino. I learned that sometimes, I have to do things I don't like so I can accomplish things I want.

As it turned out, Sabino was the best school I ever attended as far as the number of good, lifelong friends I made. No one made fun of me, at all. Instead, my friends invited me to ditch class with them or join them during lunchtime to go across the street from the school and slip into the desert to smoke pot. Back then, lots of kids smoked pot. When I was 14, I smoked for the first time with my sisters in Tami's room upstairs. Our parents had given us three joints because in those days, many parents said, "We'd rather have you do this at home where we can keep an eye on you."

I didn't think that reasoning was shocking back then. Today, if I tell people my parents gave me my first joint, they are really surprised and think it's downright wrong. However, I have met several people who described a similar scenario when recounting their first marijuana experience. Still, I must admit that if I had kids now, I wouldn't give them a joint. That said, I don't believe it harmed us as adults. My sisters and I all turned out to be productive members of society and we are not addicted to drugs. More than 30 years later, I now think of those times as just how life was in the '70s and '80s. My parents were not helicopter parents, and I'm glad they weren't. Their approach made us independent and self-sufficient.

Fitting In

My new high school friends even asked me to do things with them on the weekend. Everything that normal kids did, I was doing—it was a wonderful feeling! Finally, I had found friends who treated me like a peer, kids who didn't see me differently. That's all I ever wanted.

Tucson was the happiest part of my teenage years simply because I fit in. Sometimes, when we'd go somewhere and get out of the car, they'd say, "Teri, are you going to get out of the car"? I'd tell them, "I need my walker." Then they'd say, "Oh, god, I forgot!" We all laughed.

Freshman year I met Joanie on my first day when I was walking into English class. I was late because I decided to use my walker instead of my wheelchair. It was impossible for me to make it to all my classes in the five minutes they allowed after the bell. That first day in English class, everyone looked and the teacher stopped what she was doing and introduced me. She told me to sit wherever. Joanie said, "She can sit here."

So, I sat next to Joanie and we have been friends ever since. She introduced me to her friends, and I think because she liked me, others liked me. My physical difference was no big deal to them. Finally!

Joanie is by far one of the most honest, strong, confident girls I have ever met. I've always envied her emotional strength. A New York Italian with a great sense of humor, she says it like it is. She was raised by strong parents who stayed together. Joanie's parents were one of my favorite sets of parents.

Joanie's dad told her, "You don't need a man to get what you want."

To this day, Joanie has lived that way. She takes no one's bullshit, yet, she has a big caring heart for people. One time, Joanie told me, "We get along because we are girly girls, but we think like guys. Plus, we are both addicted to makeup."

From the beginning of our friendship, Joanie and I both felt like we didn't have a lot in common with most women. We found women harder to talk to than men, and that hasn't changed. Sometimes, I think it's because I didn't feel like a "conventional" woman. As we went through life, Joanie and I made similar choices. I don't have kids, and she didn't want kids. We both like men and sex, but just without the kid part.

Getting Into Big Trouble

Overall, I was a good kid in high school, but there was that one and only time in freshman year when I did something that, in my opinion, was bad. My friend Peri and I got to know each other through mutual friends at school. Peri was skinny, like me, but at 5' 10" she towered over me at barely 5' tall. We probably looked like the odd couple, but we got along great. Peri invited me to spend the night at her house, which ended up being a lot of fun. The next day, she had to babysit some kids down the street, so I went with her because we wanted to keep hanging out. Well, we were young and bored, and we wanted to party. Actually, we wanted to smoke pot, but we didn't have any. We searched the house for alcohol and found the liquor cabinet, stocked with everything—vodka, whiskey, rum, scotch, you name it.

We didn't know anything about liquor, so we unscrewed every bottle and poured it into a big, yellow, McDonald's supersized soda cup. The only thing we could find to use as a mixer was a little bit of grape juice left in a pitcher in the fridge. Of course, we added what was left because we thought we were so smart! Meanwhile, the kids Peri was supposed to be watching were outside playing. We chugged down the drink, about 32 ounces, even though it tasted horrible. After finishing a second supersized cup full of booze, I stretched out on the living room floor and listened to Billy Joel, lost in the music. When I had to get up off the floor to go to the bathroom, Peri helped me. Suddenly, I blacked out.

After that, I have a fuzzy memory of coming to, sitting at the end of Peri's bed, staring at a small tin trash can. Peri's dad was in the room. He was a doctor, and he put some contraption down my throat, maybe because he thought I was having a seizure and wanted to prevent me from injuring myself. Later, my family told me this part of the story because I didn't remember.

The next thing I recall is waking up in the intensive care unit of the hospital. I spent the night there with heart monitors attached to me because they thought I was having some sort of seizure related to my CP. The doctors were unaware of the large amounts of alcohol I had consumed.

My dad was the only one at the hospital who asked me if I'd been drinking. I told him, "I swear, I only had one beer."

Dad said it smelled like alcohol and he mentioned it to Peri's dad, who had assumed I was having seizures, even though I didn't have a history of seizures. People usually see me as very sweet and innocent, especially back then, and they believed I was not the type to get into trouble, specifically with alcohol or pot. Many kids in the '70s and '80s tried both, so why wouldn't I? I admit it wasn't smart, but I did it.

That day, I asked Peri to promise not to spill the beans about drinking—and she didn't. However, my blood tests came back revealing an alcohol level a little over .2 percent, a level that can result in total mental confusion, difficulty walking, blackout, and poisoning. The nurse who had been so sweet to me the night before was now more like Nurse Ratched. They finally realized I was drunk! The nurse told me, "You can tell your parents, or we will!"

Yikes! I am in big trouble, I thought. That scared me, so I told the nurse I'd tell them. When Mom came to pick me up, I started crying and told her, "I have something to tell you; I'm not having seizures...."

I paused, then my mom said, "Well, the doctors aren't sure."

I confessed. "Peri and I got drunk." Mom flipped out and started yelling at me. She even told me how expensive the ambulance was. Unfortunately, I was out during the whole ambulance ride and missed all the excitement. Mom wanted to ground me until I was 35 years old. My dad didn't agree. I remember him saying, "It's not like she can sneak out of the house."

For a long time, every night when Dad got home from work, he waved his scotch and water under my nose. Just the smell made me cringe! That was my dad's way of reminding me of my mistake.

The worst part of the whole story was I didn't see Peri again during our high school years. Her parents sent her away to a place in Texas for "bad kids." It didn't seem to matter that it wasn't just her fault—I was as much to blame as she was. I think her parents freaked out over the whole incident because I couldn't walk and I almost died. In the beginning, Peri called when she had phone privileges, and we wrote letters. But as time went by, we lost contact. This was before the internet and email.

Peri got released at 17 years old and went back to Tucson. When she got home, her parents told her they were moving to Europe, and she was on her own. Oddly enough, I found her on Facebook in 2009, and we reconnected. She had been living in Las Vegas. It made me so happy to know she was OK!

In 2010, Peri and I went to Europe and had a great time. We talked about the drinking incident and how badly I felt about it. Peri said, "It wasn't your fault; I had been getting in trouble a lot and that incident was the last straw for my parents."

No "Special Needs Kid" for Me

After my close call with alcohol, I settled into high school and more adventures with friends. I wanted to fit in so badly and be what I considered normal. I didn't want to be the special needs kid that was stuck off in the corner. Being a part of the action, like my sisters, was the driving force of my high school years. In my head, I didn't think of myself as handicapped and I wanted others to see me as fully capable, too. Mostly, I was grateful to just have friends who wanted to hang out and include me in their lives outside of school. Sabino was the school that fulfilled my need for social acceptance better than any other school I attended while growing up.

A new friend in the ninth grade was Dina, whom I had met through Peri. Dina was funny, wild, and crazy fun, and I wanted more of that in my life. Dina invited me to spend the night at her house—but it only happened once. At her sleepover, we snuck out in the middle of the night, which was a major feat for me since sneaking around was not easy given my physical challenges and the clicking sound of my walker on tile floors.

We wandered around her neighborhood—Dina walking and me in my wheelchair. When the cops saw us, Dina took off running and hid in a wash—a dry creek bed—and left me sitting in my wheelchair in the middle of the street. When the cops approached me, I told them I was out for a stroll! They must have believed me because they didn't say anything and just left. Dina was hiding in the bushes somewhere and she saw the whole exchange. Later, we snuck back into her house, undetected.

Dina's Mom didn't allow me in the house after that because she said my walker chipped the tile floors in her house. Dina told her mom my walker didn't do it—her bike did it. Still, I never was invited back into her house; instead, I'd wait at the front door.

Along with having new friends, I got lucky and had a date. In ninth grade at Sabino, a classmate, Sam, asked me to a football game. He was the little brother of one of Tami's friends. One time when I was at his house, Sam French kissed me in his bedroom and that was my first real kiss. We went to the football game and had a pretty good time, but a few days later he "broke up" with me, explaining, "People are asking why I went out with you." Then he added, "I want to date some other girls."

When Sam broke the news to me, I was sitting on the cement ledge that held the flagpole, waiting for my ride home. I knew people probably said something to him about going out with me, but I didn't think it would bother him. I was wrong. Sam left after he told me the breakup news, and I continued to wait for my ride and watch people leave school. I saw my old crush—"heel down, Tommy"—walk by. A few tears rolled down my cheeks as I thought about what had just happened. *I'll never have a boyfriend.*

I didn't run into Sam again until after high school. His family had moved out of state. Some four years later, I saw him one night at a bar, which ended in another brief interlude. More on that later.

Smart, But Treated Dumb

During my freshman year, I had a tutor for two or three days a week after school. The plan was to skip sophomore year so my twin and I would be in the same graduating class. I hated being a year behind her, especially when I knew I was as smart as Traci. I had been held back because the academic administration decided that CP meant I was mentally slow, and I needed to be in special schools. Completely misinformed and ignorant thinking about people with physical differences.

Clearly, I was not academically slow. I got better grades than my sisters. I read a wide array of literature, from Shakespeare to Steinbeck, and even though math wasn't my strongest subject, I was holding my own in algebra with help from my tutor. Karin was a college graduate in her early twenties who, once the tutoring session was over, wanted to spend time together as a friend. She got me involved in this group called Rainbows for Girls, a Masonic Youth Organization. The group facilitators taught the girls about leadership, teamwork, and community service. We raised money for different charities by having spaghetti feeds, dances, banquets, and other community events. There was a dress code; girls had to wear long dresses—a tradition that reminded me of *Little House on the Prairie*.

Rainbows for Girls was different than anything I had experienced. I met nice people, and I liked hanging out with Karin, which was like having another older sister. In this group, the older girls mentored the younger ones, which I liked, although I did not like the religious tone of the organization. Rainbows for Girls did give me a social outlet with a group of people I wouldn't have been exposed to in my everyday life. After about a year, we moved back to California and my time with this group ended.

This Will Be Good for You!

My parents had learned about Karin through an elderly, wealthy, grande dame of sorts who owned the historic, well-known Tack Room in Tucson. Her name was Fan Kane and my parents told me to call her Mrs. Kane out of respect. At 80 years old, she had dyed black hair, bobbed with bangs. Deep wrinkles and pale white skin accented her bright red lipstick that bled through the wrinkles on her lips.

She fancied herself as an expert on the handicapped, both mentally and physically. Mrs. Kane had introduced Karin to my parents, and she convinced them to enroll me in painting and piano lessons. They all decided these activities would be good for me, thinking it would increase my dexterity. So, I spent Saturdays at piano lessons or painting lessons. I liked both painting and piano, but soon realized I was not an artist or a piano player. In addition, I felt self-conscious because I knew I wasn't good at either. As for my dexterity, I thought it made zero difference. Soon, these weekly lessons turned to boredom, and I dreaded them.

Still, I was required to practice piano regularly, and occasionally, I had to go to Mrs. Kane's house—a dark and gloomy place that smelled of mothballs—to play the piano for her. She told me what I did wrong in a way that scared me—maybe something along the lines of Joan Crawford in *Mommy Dearest.* Mrs. Kane was not a warm, fuzzy, sweet woman.

One day, Tami picked me up from Mrs. Kane's after one of my lessons. When I got in the car, I started crying, telling my sister, "I hate Mrs. Kane. She makes me nervous."

Tami said, "Just tell Mom and Dad you don't want to go anymore."

I didn't tell them because I knew I'd still have to play piano and paint. My parents tended to make me do things if the professionals they talked with thought it was good for me. My parents knew I hated the piano lessons; I complained about it, but I think they were afraid of Fan Kane, too.

On the other hand, my piano teacher was a sweet lady named Mrs. Inch. She didn't yell at me and tell me I did things wrong. Instead, she taught me something on the piano. I ended up learning one song, "Someday My Prince Will Come," from *Snow White.*

My painting teacher was a high school girl, Andrea, who was sweet and smart. I did one painting of a bowl of fruit with a teakettle on a table. It turned out halfway decent, but only because Andrea guided my hand as I drew, talking to me about capturing the light on the fruit. It might have been fun if I thought I was good at either activity—but I wasn't.

My First Paid Job

While still a freshman, I decided to venture into the work world. There weren't a whole lot of employers in Tucson looking for 15-year-old girls with CP, but I got lucky. I landed a brief job as a movie extra in the movie *Stir Crazy,* starring Richard Pryor and Gene Wilder, and directed by Sidney Poitier.

My dad was the general manager at the Cadillac dealership in Tucson. When filming came to town they used cars from his dealership, and that's how we found out they needed extras. After the first day, my sisters got bored with the whole scene, but Mom and I stayed on so we would get paid. I thought, *I've hit the big time making $150 for four days of work, and I get to miss four days of school.*

During the film shoot, I met interesting people, and the actors were fun and kind. Sidney Poitier presented me with a cardboard parking pass that said, "Made Especially for Teri," and many people on the cast and crew signed it for me. One day, Gene Wilder showed up in the stands where hundreds of extras had gathered for the rodeo scene. He asked, "Is there a Teri up here?"

I was in the front row in the corner, close to where he was standing. I thought, *He must be talking about a different Teri,* so I said nothing.

My mom spoke up. "Here she is," pointing at me.

I got out of my chair so Mr. Wilder could sit. He sat down and then invited me to sit on his lap. He was wearing black leather chaps and a black vest. People started snapping pictures and asking Mr. Wilder to take pictures with them. He said, "Only for Teri." Then he whispered in my ear, "It's fucking hot up here." I cracked up laughing because it was funny that he said fuck.

Little did he know it was my favorite word.

I also had the opportunity to meet Richard Pryor, who wandered around the set in between filming, which was most of the time. One day a character actor who played a Mexican prisoner took me to lunch where the cast and crew ate. While we ate, he asked me, "What do you want to do when you grow up?"

"I want to be a model," I told him confidently.

At 15, I imagined being a model would be fun, and it was still a part of my romantic dreams. I thought, *You never see handicapped models, so I could be the first.*

I was young and naïve, but I still had my dreams.

Chapter 10

The Worst Years of High School

In summer 1980, my family moved to San Diego, which dubbed itself "America's Finest City." I soon learned that was laughable—at least in my case! As for the new school, Torrey Pines High School, the good news was that I had enough credits to start as a junior and catch up to Traci. The bad news was junior year turned out to be the worst year of my high school life.

Adjusting to a New High School

Torrey Pines is in a nice part of San Diego, but at the time I thought the students were mostly stuck up. They seemed like self-absorbed, vapid human beings—teenagers driving BMWs and Mercedes-Benzes that their parents bought them. The truth is, I felt uncomfortable being around all those kids from wealthy families. I didn't feel I was good enough and that's the impression I got from them, too—they didn't think I was good enough to be around them.

I am much more at ease in a less affluent environment with down-to-earth, working-class people. Back then, I felt unworthy because I had no friends in that environment, so other people's wealth just compounded my sense of not fitting in.

Now, as an adult, I realize not every wealthy person is like that. I'm sure there are wealthy people who are "salt of the earth" and who don't let their wealth affect them in a negative way—at least, I want to believe that.

I Need a Friend

At Torrey Pines High School I started with two friends, but they soon moved on to other friends. One became best friends with a girl labeled the "school slut." The other girl I considered to be my new friend told me, "I can't hang out with you anymore because you're in a wheelchair, and this guy I like won't like that I hang out with you."

When she said that, my gut feelings were, *You are fat, freckly, and ugly. You don't even have a charming personality, which seems to always help—but not in your case! Fine, good fucking riddance!*

I didn't say anything, but I kept wondering, *Why does she think she is any better than I am?* I never, ever said that out loud to anyone, but I thought it and felt it because her words hurt deeply and crushed my sense of self.

The kids at my school in Tucson usually liked me, and I considered myself a great friend. Peer pressure is strong, and at my new school, harsh. It felt as if everyone thought they were better than me just because I couldn't walk, despite whatever their own physical characteristics were. In my heart, I felt the same as anyone else, just physically slower; at this school, no one could see past my wheelchair.

Most of my junior year I spent at my house with no friends. I sat in my room and cried a lot that year, wishing I could go back to Tucson. After school, I went directly home and waited for my sisters so I could hang out with them. Tami, who was a senior at Torrey Pines, brought cans of Foster's beer home from her job at the Wine and Deli. If our parents weren't home, we'd play "Quarters," the drinking game. We'd take turns trying to bounce a quarter into a full glass of beer. If I missed, I had to drink the glass of beer, but if the quarter landed in the glass, I could make another participant chug the glass of beer. I was bored and this seemed like a good way to have some fun. Our parents had no idea what we were doing when they were gone, and I'm not sure they ever found out. Although, there were marks from the quarters that marred the butcher-block kitchen table.

Crushing on My Sisters' Boyfriends

Sometimes, Tami included me when she was with her boyfriend Josh. I had crushes on two of Tami's boyfriends; first Mike, and then Josh. Both were handsome and nice to me. Tami seemed happy with her boyfriends, which was hard for me to watch, especially since I didn't have even one boyfriend. I was somewhat jealous of my older sister, but not in a bad way—maybe I was envious because I wanted to know what it felt like for someone to be interested in me. Back then, I just considered Tami lucky. I couldn't wait to see what it felt like to have a guy interested in me. I thought, *I'm excited for my turn.* Sometimes in my weaker moments, I wondered if I'd ever get a turn!

Tami knew I liked her boyfriend, Mike, maybe because I told her, "Wow, Mike is a babe!"

I'm sure Tami told Mike her little sister had a crush on him, which was true because I was just all googly over him. He used to tell me, "When I get my license, I am going to take you on a date!"

Of course, I thought, *That will be so great.* I wanted it to be true!

My twin dated but didn't have steady boyfriends. Lots of guys wanted to date Traci in part because she was so beautiful, but she was picky. She usually found something wrong with them. For example, a local guy in Coronado, Edgar, liked Traci. He was slightly older and out of high school. One time he came over asking if Traci was home. My mom said she was, but she couldn't find her in her room. Edgar hung around talking to us, waiting for Traci to show up. When Edgar left, I looked in Traci's room and found her hiding in the closet! She told me, "He has zits on his back!" That was her picky excuse.

It's All in Your Head!

When I had P.E. class at Torrey Pines, this guy named Kurt started showing up at the gym, even though he wasn't in the class. It seemed a bit odd that he watched me from outside the door when I played badminton with the teacher. After class, Kurt would talk with me. Turns out he had dropped out of Torrey Pines at some point. I thought he was cute with his long brown hair; he kind of reminded me of David Cassidy from *The Partridge Family*.

Kurt started coming over to my house, just hanging out and talking. He played Led Zeppelin songs for me on his acoustic guitar in my room. I'm surprised I did not fall in love, but he did something that was a major turn off. Kurt had some screwy ideas about why I had CP. One day when we were standing in the garage at my house he said, "The reason you can't walk is because it's all in your head! Mind over matter Teri, and you can walk."

I responded, "What the fuck? Are you crazy?"

Then he said, "You just don't try hard enough."

That was the end of our brief friendship.

Invisible

I was still anxious to get a job, so I decided to volunteer at the Boys & Girls Club near our house in Solana Beach. When I told them I'd like to volunteer, they said, "Great." So, I started to show up every weekend. There was just one problem, not one member of the club staff ever asked me once to do anything. It was like I was invisible. My mom would drop me off, I'd walk in with my walker and say, "I'm here, what should I do?"

They assigned me nothing. I usually sat in a chair somewhere and watched everything going on. I kept showing up, thinking the staff would eventually give me some menial tasks. In hindsight, they probably didn't know what to do with me. Maybe they didn't want to hurt my feelings by telling me they didn't need me? It's a mystery to me.

None of the kids at the Boys and Girls Club had physical disabilities. I was the only one. But I wasn't there to participate as a customer, I was there as a volunteer to work. It was such an odd experience, especially to feel invisible. I think I lasted about a month, and then I simply quit going. I just thought, *What's the point?*

I wasn't assertive in my teenage years, but if something like that happened today, I'd definitely say something about it. At the time, I felt defeated and embarrassed—a loser.

Skiing

My sisters, Mom, and I were invited to go with Traci's high school friend Vicki and her mom on a Tahoe ski weekend. They had their own Lear jet and a house in Tahoe. It was an all-girls' weekend and I was excited to be included.

On the slopes, all of them had their ski instructor and I had a separate ski instructor, Ray. My ski instructor was good looking; he had dark hair and eyes, olive skin, and a broad smile with sparkling white teeth. Immediately, I had a crush on him, probably because I was a boy-crazy teenager.

This was the first time I had skied, and I had a blast. I loved the feeling of skiing down the mountain on actual skis, the real way. Here's how it worked: I

Teri skiing at Heavenly, South Lake Tahoe, 1981.

had my boots and skis on, and Ray had his boots and skis on. I stood up and he stood behind me, so his skis were on the outside of my skis, and I used his hands as ski poles. We started out the day on the easy kiddy run, but by the second day, Ray asked, "Do you wanna have some fun?"

I jumped at the offer. We rode the lift up the mountain to a real ski run. Once there, we took off and zipped all the way down the mountain, zigzagging and turning, flying past trees and other people! The thrill was beyond my wildest imagination, plus we didn't fall once. The only time I ever fell was when we were just standing still at the bottom of the run, talking to someone. We both had a good laugh about that!

On the last day, Ray put me on his shoulders with my skis on and we skied down the mountain with me squealing with excitement. Perhaps Ray was showing off a bit, but it is something I will remember.

At night, we played the drinking game Quarters while our moms were out doing whatever they did. When our moms came back to the house, we were all buzzed and giggling. Vicki was laughing so hard she must've done the best at Quarters—or worst—depending on how you look at it. She turned out to be the best thing in her family, bringing them lots of laughter and happiness.

We stayed in contact over the years, and Traci and Vicki stayed friends, until her death from a rare lung disease. Both of my sisters dated Vicki's older brother, but that didn't work out so well in our household. One afternoon he knocked on our door at the start of my sisters' "love triangle, teenage fighting, hair-pulling, bra snapping, and name calling" period. I answered the door and with a bit of sarcasm and a slight smile, I told him, "You are so busted."

He talked to me a lot about my sisters, trying to get a better idea of what they were thinking. Regularly, I'd tell him, "You're just crazy!"

Senior Year & Sooo Done!

We moved to Coronado Island across the bay from San Diego in my senior year. This meant another new school. Traci and I attended Coronado High School, which was somewhat better than Torrey Pines, but still a big zero on my scorecard.

In the friend department, I did better at the new high school. My new friends at Coronado hung out with me at lunch, but none of them spent time with me on the weekends. They were friends with my sisters, too, so that helped. My sisters started taking me to parties with them, and at least I had a bit of a social life in my senior year. Basically, I became a party girl. Before long, I got to be known as the "beer bong queen" because I was good at drinking. I could hold my own, even though I only weighed about 80 pounds. I didn't smoke pot much my senior year, but I drank.

Lots of kids in high school in the '70s and '80s were smoking pot and/or drinking. I was no exception. When there were parties, there was lots of beer, booze, and pot around, among other things. When I first showed up at parties, people seemed surprised to see me. I guess the stereotype was that teens with physical handicaps didn't party; but once I was there, people talked to me and laughed. Many kids stood next to me and by the end of the night, I'd have people leaning on my walker to help them stay standing.

I wish I could say I was just trying to be cool and fit in, but I truly liked going to the parties, laughing and talking to people. Now, when I think about it, the party scene was a good way for me to show people that I am just like anyone else. To this day, I like to have a good time and feel like I am in on the fun.

Awful Comments

In senior year, I became more accepted, and people genuinely talked to me when they saw me. Perhaps some people who may have thought of me as different or weren't sure what to say or how to relate to me, realized that I am not that different. It has always been very odd to me when people say they have to "get used to me," or they are not sure what to say. "Hi," is a good start.

Still, there were some kids at these parties—older kids not in high school—who said stupid things, like, "You're Tami and Traci's sister? They are so pretty," or "You're pretty, too bad you can't walk."

People were just trying to be nice, but sometimes the way things came out of their mouths, it sounded awful. A lot of the time, I laughed about it because the comments were just awful and obnoxious. While laughing, I'd be thinking, *I can't believe they said that!*

"You're pretty for a crippled girl." That was my favorite stupid comment because it was like I was pretty for a crippled girl, but ugly for a regular girl? Or they were just so surprised that I could be pretty and have CP at the same time?

At times, I wanted to say, "Gee, thanks for the fucking compliment!"

Sometimes, I did.

Depending on my mood, I'd either say, "Thank you," or "I know, Tami and Traci are beautiful, but what am I? Chopped liver?" Sometimes, I'd just let it go, trying to be humorous and not bitchy. I liked to make people laugh; it made them feel more at ease.

Figuring Out Boys

I kinda had a date with this guy, Brad, a classmate who regularly walked into my art class and talked to some guys that sat at my table. He didn't really talk to me, but he was checking me out. One day, he visited the store where Tami worked and asked her, "Do you think Teri will go out with me?"

Tami told Brad to ask me out. When Tami told me what she said to him, I said, "Oh my god! I'm not going! I don't even like him that way!"

But my sisters just wanted me to go out on a date, so they insisted. I thought, *If he's so great, why don't one of you go out with him?*

Well, Brad took me out to dinner and then dessert for mud pie, which ended up being the best part of the date. We smoked some pot, and he tried to kiss me. I was nervous; I didn't really know him, and I wasn't attracted to him. Brad was a nice guy, just not for me. After that arranged date, I decided I liked choosing my own boys.

When I saw a guy I thought was cute or funny, I crushed on him like any other typical teenager. Mostly, I lived vicariously through my sisters. They talked to me about boys, and they knew which ones I liked. Unfortunately, no boys I was interested in ever asked me out.

No one asked me to the senior prom. At the time, I was so bummed because I felt like I was missing out on a major high school event. I wanted to get glammed up and wear a nice dress. It's not like I wanted to dance; I just wanted to dress up, party, and stay out all night. Traci had gone to her junior prom at Torrey Pines with a boyfriend, and Tami had gone to her senior prom at Torrey Pines. She got to stay in a hotel room with a bunch of friends. It sounded like so much fun and looked like a big deal.

In my case, I could have gone as a single person with a group of friends, but I didn't have close enough friends for that option. Instead, I stayed home that evening. If I had still lived in Tucson, the prom scenario would have ended with a much different outcome. On a positive note, at least I don't have any of those dated prom photos haunting me in my later years. Now, I'd probably cringe at my dress or my '80s hairdo.

Getting Out of High School

It turns out, Coronado High School counted credits differently than my high school in Tucson. According to Coronado standards, I was far behind on my credits, so I had to take a full load of classes during the day in addition to night classes so I'd have enough credits to graduate on time.

The whole time I was pushing hard to get the necessary credits, the high school principal told me I wasn't going to make it. He said that I could graduate the following January. I refused to accept this. I thought, *No one graduates in January! That will make me seem like a real loser.*

I decided there was no way I was going to graduate late, so I pushed and worked hard. Just a few days before graduation, the school told me I had made it. I must admit I really did enjoy proving the principal wrong! Determination has always been my strength.

I couldn't wait to get out of high school, even though I had no idea what I was going to do with my life. In

June 1982, I graduated, and it was one big non-event. There was a school-sponsored party at a rec center where the high school seniors watched a slide show of all the popular classmates. There wasn't one photo of me included in the show. I was invisible. No one talked to me at the party, so I went home after the slideshow. Even though my twin was there, too, I didn't hang out with her—Traci had plans with friends. That last high school event was a letdown, but I was so happy to be free from school.

Years later, whenever my sisters and I talk about the high school years and I tell them how bad it was for me, they say, "That was high school."

Of course, I know that, but those kinds of experiences stuck with me. My sisters don't understand because they didn't have to deal with few or no friends. Every school we went to my sisters were popular and made lots of friends. They were considered very pretty, nice girls, which is absolutely true. I wanted to be like them, yet I don't think they will ever know how sick and tired I got with people coming up to me and saying, "You are Tami and Traci's sister? They are so pretty."

I have learned that people just don't think that being pretty can be connected to having CP. Even now, when someone tells me I'm pretty, the old high school stuff still whispers in the back of my head. Sometimes, I have difficulty believing I am pretty, or I think they are just being nice. I believe that is why I am concerned with wearing makeup and making sure my clothes look stylish. I'm sure there will always be that self-doubting voice in the back of my mind.

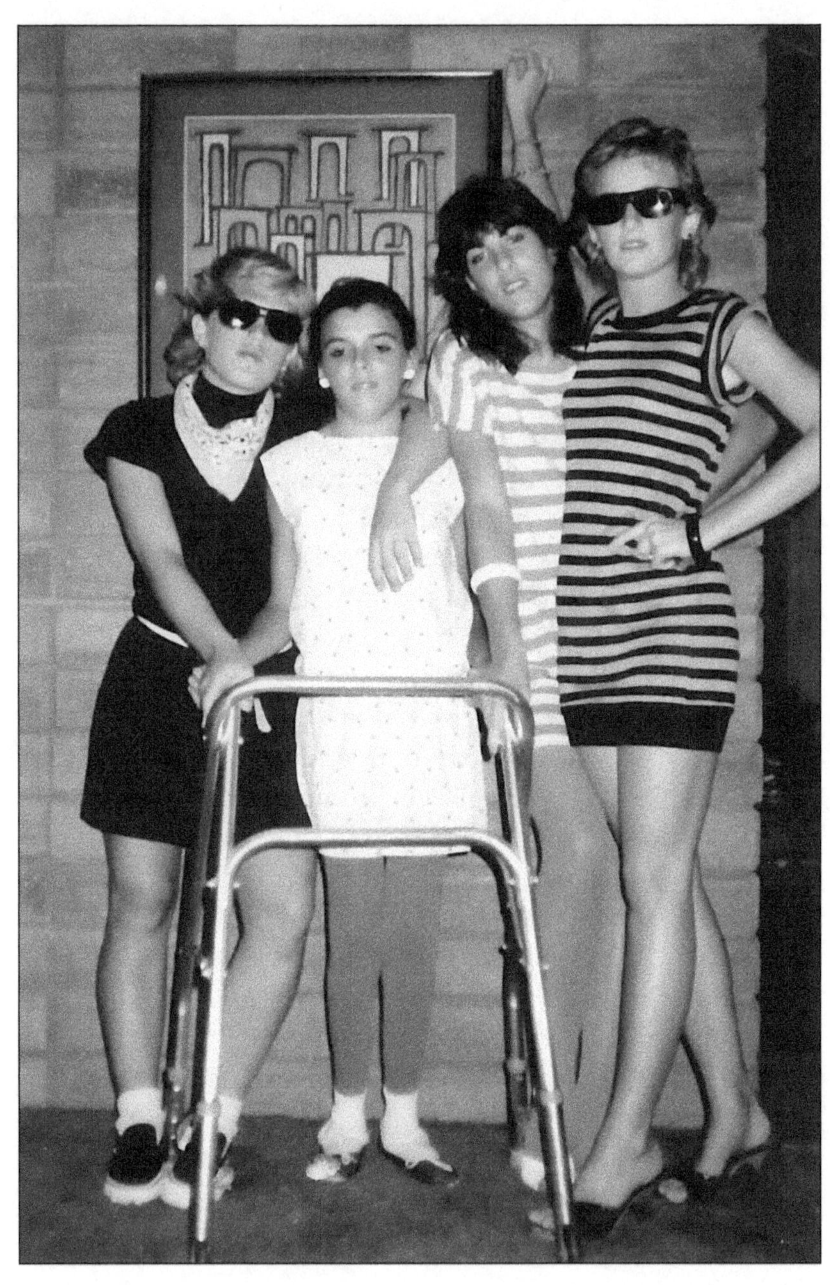

Trying to "get the look" with our friend Krissy (left), Teri, Traci, and Tami (right). Teri is about 17 years old.

Chapter 11

Wanted: Boyfriends, Sex, and a Job

As far back as I can remember, I have been boy crazy. Having cerebral palsy (CP) made it difficult for me as a teenager to even get a date. Even if I was as beautiful as say, Angelina Jolie, it would be hard to get a date if I walked into the room with CP. Trust me. I think it is easier to be a man with a physical handicap and get dates since many women like to mother and take care of men. On the other hand, most men like to have a trophy girlfriend or a beautiful wife on their arm who will dote on them or be their nurse if they need to be taken care of. In the relationship department, my romantic future wasn't looking too promising.

My First Date

My first real date was right after high school graduation with a guy named Jake who was about 22 years old. He had a VW van with a bed in the back, which made me a bit nervous because I'd hear my dad's warning in my head: "You are not allowed to go out with guys in vans."

So, on our first date when I walked outside and saw Jake's van, I thought, *Just my luck.*

Expecting my dad to object, I was surprised when he let me go on the date. He shook Jake's hand and with a smile on his face said, "Have a good time!"

I think Dad was just glad I finally got a date! So, off I went in a cool, VW hippie van. My dad didn't shake any boy's hand who came over to take out one of my sisters. He just ignored them and walked out of the room. When asked about it, Dad only said he knew what they all wanted: "I was a teenage boy, too."

Imagine my shock when I watched my dad shake Jake's hand. It was both laughable and surprising!

I knew Jake from going to parties at his house on Coronado Island, along with my sisters. It was his house where I first did a beer bong. His sister had won Miss Coronado a year earlier. I knew about this because Traci was in the Miss Coronado pageant twice. The first time, my twin won Miss Congeniality, and the second year she won first runner up in the pageant. I remember Traci telling me that we should be in the pageant together. At the time, it seemed impossible to me. I laughed and told her, "Pageants are not my thing, at all. I am far too self-conscious for that kind of attention."

On our date, Jake took me to dinner and then back to his house. We sat on the couch, drank beer, and talked. Nothing happened. At one point, he said he was tired, but I was totally clueless about what that implied, so I responded, "Oh, I'm fine."

In hindsight, I now see that I probably could have had sex that night, which was something I was curious about, but I blew it. Nothing more happened after that date. He didn't ask me out again, but a year or so later we met up—and another opportunity would arise!

A Real Job

While I was longing for a boyfriend, I also wanted a real job. A couple months out of high school I heard about this program that helped people with physical or mental disabilities find jobs. There was a group of us who were enrolled in the program. I was the only one who couldn't walk independently. By then, I used my walker almost exclusively unless I was at the mall or somewhere that required lots of walking, then I used my wheelchair. Everyone else in the program had other kinds of disabilities, including intellectual.

We all got jobs at Balboa Naval Hospital, but I was the only one to get a job working in the x-ray department at the front desk. Everyone else in the group got jobs in the cafeteria. I got the best gig! Later, the program staff moved me to the ultrasound department where I had my own small office. I filed charts, answered phones, scheduled appointments, and talked to patients about how to prepare for an ultrasound. Soon, I was reading the scan reports over the phone to doctors who called needing results. I met lots of people and the people I worked with were supportive. My co-workers and the patients liked me, and I was good at my work. Quickly I became the model employee; I was punctual and didn't miss a day.

One day this little old man with a gravelly voice and crotchety demeanor came in to make an appointment. When he saw me, he said to one of the techs in the office, "What? The Navy hiring child labor now?"

We all laughed, then I said, "I'm 18," acting like I was 37 or something.

Even though I loved that job, there were a couple things that were wrong. It ended after six months, and I didn't get paid for doing the job. The department wanted to keep me, but couldn't get funding to create the job opening, so I was let go. I'm sure they eventually got funding since the need for ultrasounds kept growing. At least that job gave me some good work experience, and I had something to put on a resume.

Just after high school, Tami, Teri, Traci, 1982.

While I was in the job, my parents asked more than once, "Why do it if you aren't getting paid?"

They didn't understand why this job was so important to me, even without the pay. I liked the work and the feeling of being productive and appreciated. Besides, I thought, *What else do I have to do at this point in my life?*

Back to Tucson

In summer 1983, right before turning 19, my mom, dad, and I moved back to Tucson. Happy days were here again!

My dad lost his job in San Diego, but we still had the house in Tucson, which my parents had rented out. He got a job at a Pontiac dealership, so we moved back. My sisters didn't want to leave the San Diego area, so they stayed. Tami lived with her boyfriend, Fred, and Traci lived in a house with a couple of roommates. San Diego had become their home base.

I didn't have a job, so my parents gave me money when I needed it. My job search continued in Tucson, but back then it was hard as hell to find one. The job interviewer would see me with my walker and immediately ask, "What's wrong"? And then ask, "What can you do?"

Obviously, this was frustrating because I applied for jobs I could do, like receptionist or office clerk. I wasn't applying to be a waitress or a construction worker.

Hanging Out at Bars

All my friends still lived in Tucson and the drinking age was 19 in Arizona, so I thought, *This is the greatest thing ever! Good to be back in Tucson!*

Even though I turned 19 before any of my friends, I looked the youngest, so my friends were all happy because they figured if I could get into a bar, they wouldn't even get carded. That's exactly what happened. Plus, everyone liked my handicapped parking permit. I didn't drive at the time, but I had a parking permit that I took with me when riding in other people's cars.

For a year straight, I went out every single night but one. During the day I attended community college and partied at night. My friends and I figured out the specials at every bar for each night of the week. One night might be "Ladies Night," or maybe "Nickel/Dime Night," or "Margarita Night." On the weekends, well, because it was the weekend, we went out. That year was one of the best in my young life, filled with fun. I felt like I was making up for all the boring, lonely, California years of my youth.

Sometimes, when I met a guy at a bar, he'd ask me if I was one of "Jerry's Kids." I'd have to explain that multiple sclerosis (MS) is not cerebral palsy (CP). People don't really know the difference. I got tired of explaining that with MS you can die young, but with CP, you don't.

When strangers saw me walk into a bar with my walker, a lot of times they thought I'd been in a car accident. They'd say, "You are too pretty to be crippled." This was followed with shocked looks on their faces when I explained I was born like this. It's odd how people assume, or think, people who have physical disabilities must be ugly.

There were times when we were at a bar and some guys physically picked me up—I only weighed about 75 to 80 lbs.—and walked out of the bar with me. Since I couldn't jump up and run away, or give them a swift kick, I felt vulnerable and defenseless. Usually, a guy asked if he could pick me up to help me get up or down the stairs. However, one guy grabbed me without my permission, carried me out of the bar and headed to his car. My friend Joanie took off her shoes and ran after him, hitting his shoulders with her stiletto heal, yelling, "Put her down or I'll scream for the cops."

He finally put me down. I was scared and feared for my safety. Now, it seems kind of funny, but still, I was lucky nothing more happened.

Another time, I was dancing with a guy at a bar, having a good time. Unless I was super wasted, I didn't dance. Plus, I think the song was "Pour Some Sugar on Me" by Def Leppard, and when you're drunk, that's a good dance song!

After the song ended, he asked me to dance again, but I said no since my friends and I decided to leave the bar. This guy and two of his friends followed us to our car. We got inside, locked the doors, and they started banging on the windows. The bouncers came out and warned these guys they were going to call the police. They backed off, but the whole way home we were afraid they'd follow us. That was the last time I went to that bar.

A Chance to Have Sex

During that wild year in Tucson, I ran into Sam again, the one I had my first kiss with. He was the one who decided he couldn't go out with me anymore after one date because his friends were asking him why he was going out with me. We saw each other at a bar and started chatting. After a while, we went to his car and made out. Just kissing. He invited me to his friend's apartment, and I decided to go. Sam kept trying to convince me to have sex with him. I was a virgin, and I didn't want him to be my first experience. At one point, Sam took my walker out of the room so I couldn't leave, then pulled his pants down and tried to make me give him a blowjob. I refused. "Bring my walker back, or I'll start screaming," I demanded. He did. I just kept thinking, *What an asshole.*

Sam seemed to be a nice kid in high school, so I was shocked when he did that. Days later, I saw him again when I was out with my friends. He tried apologizing. I listened to his apology, but just stared at him, like it meant nothing to me. He said goodbye and I never saw him again.

The First Time

When I was 19, I had sex for the first time. Back then I thought I was so old! It was with a guy named Max who was crazy about my twin Traci. Max was trying to get me to make Traci go out with him. We both had a mutual friend, so the three of us started hanging out regularly and drinking at bars. We got to know one another, and he started flirting with me a lot, saying, "You are pretty and you're such a cool girl."

This went on for a few months. We'd go out with my friend, whom Max was screwing at the time, but not dating. They were more like "friends with benefits" or "fuck buddies." Secretly, Max held my hand under the table and whispered things in my ear. One night, Max said he'd give me a ride home. He drove to this hill on the east side of town that overlooked the city. We were in his mom's '69 Camaro, which made me laugh because of the sexual connotation. I was buzzed and Max said he liked me and wanted to kiss me.

Eventually, I took my dress off and he said, "You have amazing tits." I thought, *Who doesn't at 19? And what 22-year-old boy wouldn't think any tits are amazing?*

Honestly, I made the decision to have sex with Max because I really thought this would be the one and only chance I'd get. That doesn't say much for my self-esteem at the time.

We did it in the passenger's seat. He was sitting and I sat on his lap, facing him. Doing it in the front bucket seat of a '69 Camaro isn't easy when you are crippled. Actually, I don't think it's easy for anybody. Luckily, I am five feet tall and only weigh about 80 pounds. That first time was only memorable because it was my first time. I didn't have an orgasm, but I do remember it feeling good.

That night I went home with my nylons in my dress pocket. When I walked through the front door it was kind of like a "walk of shame," but I was happy because I had finally done it. But I was also stupid because I did not use any birth control or protection, and Max didn't even mention it. We were irresponsible all around. Of course, using birth control didn't occur to me until much later. In addition, this was right at the time when HIV/AIDS was popping up. Yikes!

Later, I learned I can't take the pill or use patches because I have bad circulation in my legs and these forms of birth control can cause blood clots. When I had sex, I used condoms, or I had the guy pull out, thinking that worked. This form of birth control I called "cross your fingers and hope!"

The very next night after having sex with Max, I was out with my friends and ran into him. When I saw him, he acted like nothing had happened and he introduced me to his new girlfriend! My feelings were hurt, but I didn't say anything. I just thought, *Wow, that's pretty ballsy.*

I shook the new girlfriend's hand and greeted her. Max whispered in my ear, "I really like you."

At the time I thought, *Whatever!* At 19, I didn't realize or understand his game of manipulation.

This whole scene shocked me, wondering, *Why doesn't he treat me nicer?* But then again, I had no romantic thoughts of us suddenly becoming a couple. I thought so little of myself and my self-worth that I truly believed

I'd never get another chance. I questioned, *Who would want to sleep with me? Or date me? Or love me?*

After that experience with Max, those doubts with my self-worth became more predominant. Sometimes, I still question my self-worth, but I try to tell myself, I'm a good catch. Besides, I don't need anyone to support me financially. And I'm a good, thoughtful person with a great sense of humor.

Fine, Not Fine!

Not long after that, I was at a party and saw Max again. He was stinking drunk. We started talking and he told me, "I was talking with my mom about you, and I told her, 'I really like Teri, but I don't think I could handle Teri not being able to walk.'"

Then Max leaned over and whispered in my ear, "I will always love you."

I just laughed and said, "Everything's fine," even though nothing was fine.

So many times I just had to brush off things like this and act like everything was ok, even though my heart got bruised a little more each time. It pissed me off, but I didn't show it. I didn't want to seem weak, and I didn't want the guy who was rejecting me to see how he hurt me.

This became a recurring theme in my future—agreeing to sex because I thought it might be my last time and then get jilted afterward. Silly, young, and dumb! Fortunately, I wised up over time and started to realize there's a good chance I will have sex again at some point, so I don't need to do it just because an opportunity arises. (No pun intended.)

I had a couple more dates in Tucson. One was with a tall, dark, and handsome man, Gus, who had thick, dark, wavy hair. I met him in a bar after he sent pitchers of Margaritas over to my table. Weeks later, he invited me out and we ended up going on a date to the movies. While standing in line, two girls walked by us. I heard them say, "He's cute. Why is he with her?"

Throughout my life there have been times when I have heard people say something like this, especially when I'm out with a man. It has been my experience that girls are generally way meaner to me than guys. As a result, I find it easier and more fun to have guy friends than girlfriends. However, the girlfriends I do have are cool, and they have been loyal for many years.

Well, I ended up having sex with this Gus, too! We were supposed to go out again, but something odd happened. His hippie roommate with hair like ZZ Top called me and said Gus was going to be late on a day outing we had planned to Mt. Lemmon. This was a popular destination with an observatory at the top of a mountain over 9,000-feet high. The roommate said he would pick me up and we would meet Gus at Mt. Lemmon. That sounded fine to me, so I rode with his roommate to the mountaintop. We were drinking vodka in a strawberry-flavored frozen fruit drink called eegee's, popular in the Tucson area. We sat on the ground, looking at the view, talking, and drinking. Nothing happened between us, we just waited. Gus was a no show. I got a call a few days later. Apparently, the roommate told Gus things happened that didn't. When I told Gus nothing happened, he didn't believe me, and that was the end of our short-lived romance.

Back to San Diego

My partying in Tucson only lasted a year because after that, I moved. My mom and dad divorced—again—because my dad had another affair. He was a busy guy. It was so uncomfortable being in the house with my parents when their marriage was ending. When they initially fought, there was lots of yelling. After that, it could be weeks of complete silence between the two of them. They could be in the same room and still, they'd ask me to ask the other one a question. Ridiculous.

In my opinion, they were two people who should not have been married. Oddly, I think they still loved each other because they hated each other so much. Very strong feelings between those two.

Luckily, I had good friends to hang out with. My friend Steve would carry me into my house through the sliding glass door in my bedroom so my parents wouldn't hear my walker clicking on the ceramic tiling when I came home at night, way too late.

Mom would say, "This isn't a hotel"! This made me laugh, happy to get yelled at for never being home. Something about it felt very normal.

Mom and I moved back to Coronado Island in 1984, and I enrolled in San Diego City College. This time, I got much better grades, holding a 3.25 GPA. Of course, with no friends and no math classes, my GPA was bound to go up! All my classes were in writing because I hated math. The school's literary magazine published my poems and a story I wrote. One poem was about a guy who stood me up for cocaine. Now, when I look at those stories I wrote in college, I think they are horrible, but at least I was writing.

During this lonely time, I ran into Jake again. I was at a bar with Traci and one of her friends. Jake joined us and he told Traci he'd give me a ride home because she wanted to leave and I wanted to stay. I ended up going to Jake's apartment. This time, we did have sex.

After that, we never saw each other again. It was fine. I think we were mutually disinterested. Maybe it was one of those things where he was curious to see what it was like to have sex with a crippled girl. Again, as with Max, back then I did it because I honestly thought that it would probably be my last chance, so I better do it while I can. There was nothing memorable about sex with Jake. I was still young and naïve and obviously, still lacking any self-esteem or boys genuinely being attracted to me.

While I was attending San Diego Community College, I rode the city bus. One morning, I got on the bus using my walker and paid the fare that people with disabilities are allowed to pay. The driver looked at me with my walker and said, "I have to see your card that says you are disabled."

By then, I'd been riding the bus for quite some time. No one ever told me I needed a card. "My card?" *Is there a card that says 'handicapped?'*

Then she asked, "How do I know you are disabled?"

"Well," I answered, "I could let go of this walker and fall down right here. Would that help?"

Was she fucking kidding me? I thought in total disbelief.

The bus driver argued with me for a few minutes as the other passengers sat, patiently waiting to get on with their day. She threatened to throw me off the bus. I just took a seat and got off at my regular stop. Silently, I fumed, once more sitting on my anger.

Later, I ended up hiring a woman to drive me to school in her VW bug because I was tired of dealing with public transportation. I was on Supplemental Security Income (SSI), giving half the money to my mom for rent. Unfortunately, I soon realized my new driver wasn't playing with a full deck. She'd drive to her apartment after school instead of taking me home. Randomly, in the middle of a conversation, she'd start explaining something that we weren't even talking about. Then she'd start demanding more money from me. This was one more example of what I have always said: "It's expensive to be crippled!"

During this same time, Traci got in a car accident. She had a concussion and had quite a bit of mental confusion. A counselor came to the house and asked her questions about her life. She told him she went to San Diego City College. When I heard that, I said, "That's me!"

For a while, Traci thought she was me. Traci worked at a medical sales business and during her recovery for a few weeks, I ended up working Traci's job. I typed letters, answered phones, and did general secretarial duties. I didn't care much for the work, but what made it worse is her employer didn't pay me for working. Once again, not paid! I began to see a pattern.

I applied for jobs that I knew I could perform, but when I went in for the interview, the potential employer would take one look at me and say, "What can you do?"

Once again, I had to explain my office skills and note that I had attended college. Then the interviewer would tell me, "I'm sorry, we don't have anything for you."

Frustrated, one time I sarcastically said, "It's not like I'm applying for a construction job. I can answer the telephone." I didn't get that job.

Despite my loneliness, I lasted in Coronado another year, when I decided I needed a life change. I called Nana and Bapa in Oregon and asked, "If I move back to Portland, can Kelly and I rent your house?"

They said, "Of course, honey!"

I bought my one-way plane ticket to Portland in June 1985 and headed to my new life with all my life savings—about $1,000.

The night before I left for Portland, a friend from Coronado, Jerry, asked me out. He cooked shark for dinner along with a salad and beer. Afterward, we went to see *Rambo*. We had a good time and later, after I left San Diego, he told Traci, "I like Teri, but I can't handle how people stare at her in public."

Teri with her Nana and Bapa.

That night Jerry and I went to the movie I didn't notice anything unusual, but obviously Jerry did. Perhaps I had just blocked out anyone staring at me.

By this point in my life, any dates I had were a one-time deal. No guy asked me out twice—ever. Often, I thought, *I will never have a real romantic relationship.*

That thought made me so sad and lonely. I wanted romance and a future with someone who loved me for me. Being alone my whole life was not something I wanted.

Chapter 12
Oregon Bound

The next day, I gladly boarded the plane, ready to leave my old life behind and ready for a fresh start in Portland. My friend Kelly and I immediately moved into a house my grandparents allowed us to rent.

We were the only ones among our friends with our own house, so we became the party house. That first year in Portland was a blast. I had just turned 21, the legal drinking age in Oregon, so it was pretty much a nonstop blur of keg parties at our house. At times, there could be 100 people or more who showed up to party and maybe we knew 10 to 15 of them.

Before long, we started charging people to get into our house parties and that helped us buy more beer, alcohol, or whatever we wanted. My grades at Mt Hood Community College suffered during this time since I was majoring in partying.

The Guy Next Door

The people who lived in the rental next door had a business fixing up cars and selling them. A man named Matt painted the cars and my cousin Rodney, a high school student, helped him detail them. Rodney and Matt became good friends and at times, he seemed like a second dad to Rodney.

When I was still living in San Diego, Rodney would call and tell me about Matt. "He is a funny, crazy, Italian guy and I think you'd like him, Teri."

So, when I first saw Matt, I thought, *Great looking!*

He was 40 years old, about 5' 8" tall, and he had a dark tan. Basically, he was a swarthy, stocky, handsome Italian with big biceps, salt and pepper hair, and a mustache. He drove around town in a 1982 red Jeep CJ-5, looking cool with a bandana tied on his head. Later, I learned he'd mix up baby oil with iodine and rub it all over himself to get that deep tanned look. This was long before tanning booths were on every corner, or for that matter, sunscreen.

During my first year in Portland, I casually got to know Matt because I saw him next door every day. Sometimes he'd come over for a beer and just shoot the breeze. It didn't take long before I had a huge crush on him. Surprise! I'd play music extra loud, maybe something like Whitney Houston's "How Will I Know," hoping Matt heard the song's message. Sometimes, I'd go next door and ask him to oil my walker wheels because they squeaked, or they didn't roll. He'd take off the wheels and get dog hair or string out of them. Later, I learned that during this whole time Rodney had been telling Matt I was in love with him.

When I went to my college classes, I'd leave my walker in the driveway but take my wheelchair. About a year after I had met Matt, I came home from school one day and found a piece of masking tape on my walker that said, "Foxy Lady." The tape had primer all over it. I asked my roommates, "Oh my god! Who did that?"

By then, Kelly and I allowed our friend Tom to stay at our house, and he slept in the attic room. When I asked who left the note, Tom smirked and said, "Who do you think it is? It's got primer—it's Matt!"

I thought, *No way!* The idea of him flirting made me so happy I couldn't stop smiling.

The Beginning of Romance

A week or so later, I was visiting my aunt, who is Rodney's mom. We sat at a small dining table in the living room and Rodney joined us, doing his homework. The phone rang and about a minute later, Rodney told me, "Teri, Matt's coming over."

That news made me all giggly, but then I immediately freaked out and rushed to put on some makeup. A short time later, he showed up and joined us, joking and talking, and drinking tequila with us. Not wanting to miss anything, Rodney stayed in the room, pretending to do more homework. I knew my cousin planned this little meeting. They were both teasing me and giving me shit, as usual. Then suddenly, Matt looked at me and said, "So, I hear you want to stick your tongue down my throat."

I laughed nervously and responded, "I have no idea what you're talking about!"

Rodney got up and walked into the kitchen, laughing, as if he knew that was his cue to exit. Then Matt leaned over and gave me a big fat kiss! After that, we just looked at each other and laughed. I had wanted to kiss him for almost a year, and it was better than I had expected.

We ended up getting super wasted on tequila and Matt wrote his name on the back of my hand in black ink. At some point, Rodney came back into the living room and took some photos of the two of us goofing around. In one photo I'm sitting on Matt's lap, laughing, wearing his sunglasses. I had liked those sunglasses—a pair of red gargoyles—so they eventually became mine.

That night, he gave me a ride home from my aunt's house and parked his Jeep on the side of my house where no one could see it. We were drunk, but we made it inside. Later, Kelly came home and stood outside my bedroom door saying, "Nice parking job Matt!"

We were laughing behind the closed doors, having a great time. He went crazy for my boobs and my butt—seemingly not bothered or distracted by CP. He genuinely seemed to like me and my body very much.

That was the beginning of our six-year, romantic relationship. Not everyone was happy that I was with Matt, but I was fucking ecstatic because he was the first guy I really liked who liked me back—and didn't leave after one date.

My First True Love

A couple weeks after our first night together, Matt came over during one of our smaller parties. He knew I had a plane ticket to move back to San Diego. I was only planning on staying in Portland for one year and that time was just about up. We went in the bathroom to talk and he asked, "Will you stay in Portland and be with me?"

"What about my ticket?"

He said, "Who cares!"

I started crying. I'm an easy crier because I'm such a romantic and it felt like Matt had swept me off my feet. This rush of good feelings was new, and I loved it. No wonder people are always chasing love.

When I told Kelly about my plan to move in with Matt, she wasn't happy because she thought he was an alcoholic. She once told me, "You will only be his whore."

Without missing a beat, I replied, "Perfect."

I must admit, it hurt my feelings that my best friend said that; Kelly knew how much I liked Matt. I knew she was just looking out for me, but at the time it really stung my heart.

For once, I was happy to feel loved by someone I liked. I thought, *If all he wants is a whore, he could certainly find someone better than me.*

Kelly moved out to attend college in Ashland and I moved in with my aunt and uncle for about a month. Then I moved into Matt's house. I considered him my first true love.

My parents weren't happy about my new boyfriend because Matt was 19 years older than me. At one point, my dad called and asked me, "Teri, what's going on with you and this guy? Isn't he too old for you?"

In turn, I asked my dad, "How old is your current girlfriend?"

Guess what? She was 19 years younger than my dad. When I pointed this out, he said, "I guess I can't say much."

My dad said I had the best head on my shoulders, and I made good decisions. As it turned out, he never met Matt over the course of our six-year relationship.

Lots of Sex

Matt worked during the day, and I stayed home and kept myself busy. My grades were so bad I decided to quit college. Plus, I had no money to pay for it, and I wasn't interested. He'd come home from work, and we'd have lots of sex and drink. Sometimes, we stayed up until early morning having sex. Matt was the first guy I had an orgasm with—no wonder I liked him so much!

After an all-nighter, we'd end up in the kitchen and make a big meal and munch out. Those early days were so fun, which seems to be the case for most new relationships. Maybe that's why people chase that feeling so much—they're looking for something new and exciting, trying to recapture the excitement they had when they first fell in love.

To this day, when I'm in love, I want to dote and take care of a guy, no problem. It's just that every physical activity takes me so fucking long to do. Any man I want to dote over will either starve to death or fall asleep by the time I can do something for him. If I'm in the middle of stripping for fun before having sex, and my man is waiting for me to get my clothes off in a sexy way without looking all spastic, well, this could take awhile.

By the way, spastic cerebral palsy describes the most common type of cerebral palsy. I can have stiff muscles and involuntary muscle movements—spasticity—that affect my movements. It can certainly affect my stripper moves!

Anybody who chooses to be with me has got to be a little more evolved, have some patience, and definitely, have a sense of humor—all are a *must.* Early on in our relationship, Matt had all those qualities. He was also the first man to ever tell me I was sexy. It felt great when he'd say, "You have a perfect body from the knees up."

When he said that, I'd laugh, and then he'd laugh. We both knew my legs were not my best feature—but other than that, he said my body was perfect. To this day, that still makes me smile.

In 1987, *Playboy* published an issue featuring a young woman, Ellen Stohl, who was a paraplegic. She was the first disabled woman to appear in a *Playboy* nude pictorial. Matt subscribed to the magazine and when he saw the spread, he said, "You are so much prettier than she is."

When I looked at the pictures, I thought, *She's pretty. Good for her!*

People don't think of disabled people as sexual, but I am here to attest that they are! This feature in *Playboy* broke through lots of stereotypes about people with physical disabilities and their sexuality. Most able-bodied people can't handle it. I think it just scares them. Any time someone with a disability is shown in a normal way, it makes me happy. It's the way life should be.

At the time, I was about 22 and I knew my breasts were shaped like cannonballs—a highly desirable feature in *Playboy,* according to Matt. That was not something I thought about for myself. Matt wanted me to submit my photos, saying, "You could be in *Playboy.*"

I was flattered by the suggestion, but it wasn't meant to be. Interestingly, Ellen Stohl went on to be a college professor, lecturing worldwide on sexuality and body image for those with physical disabilities.

For the first couple years with Matt, I stayed home, and he worked. We hung out with friends and went on road trips to Reno. As a young twenty-something, I thought this was great fun. Matt promised, "I will take care of you forever."

In time, I learned that wasn't the last time I'd hear that statement. Too bad it's rarely true.

I often thought, *Forever is a long, long time.*

So, after a couple years with Matt and being a "homemaker," I decided it was time to get a job in case forever didn't last.

Good times for Teri and family at cousin Rodney's wedding in 1991.

Chapter 13
Getting a Job

One day while I was sitting at home watching the news, I thought, *What do I want to do with my life? I'm already 23 years old.*

The answer: I wanted to find a real job.

As I watched the news, pondering my future, a story about the Bonneville Power Administration (BPA) in Portland came on. Immediately, I thought, *That might be a good job.*

The next day, not knowing how to go about applying for a job at the BPA, I looked up the number in one of those old phone directories referred to as yellow pages. I called and was hooked up with a woman, Elaine, in the Human Resources Department whose job was to try to get disabled people hired. She mailed me a huge application that went on for about 15 pages. As soon as I got it, I filled it out and mailed it back to Elaine. We ended up having several phone conversations during my job hunt. Elaine submitted my application for job openings that she thought I was qualified for. This went on for a few months.

A Real Job

In May 1988, Elaine submitted my application for a clerk-typist position in the Finance and Budget Office. I had no idea what that was, but it sounded good. I heard nothing for a week or so. Not knowing any better, I kept calling to see when interviews started. A man named Mark finally called back and said that they didn't plan on interviewing yet. He thought I sounded anxious, so he asked if I'd like to come in and talk to him. Two days later, I had my first interview with Mark.

The interview went well, maybe because I didn't think it was the "real" one. He was just talking to me because I was impatient. Mark asked why I wanted to work at BPA. I was honest and said, "I don't make very much on SSI." Then I added, "Plus, I have a shopping problem I need to support."

We both laughed. Mark asked what I liked to do, and I told him I liked to write. He wanted me to send him something I had written. During the interview, Mark told me the BPA, which is part of the federal government's Department of Energy, was slow about hiring and I probably wouldn't hear anything for some time. Still, I remained confident about the interview. When I got home, I dropped in the mail to Mark a story I had written for a college class. I didn't think it was very good, but he liked it.

About a week later, I got a call for another interview at BPA. The woman on the phone said Mark was impressed with me and his boss, Chuck, now wanted to interview me for the clerk-typist position. A couple days later, I had an interview with Chuck, who was the head of Finance and Budget. He was probably in his late 30s and notably handsome with salt and pepper hair. He had a well-appointed office with glass windows that looked out on the rest of the larger office filled with cubicles. While I was in Chuck's office for the interview, he kept his door open. In the middle of the interview, a man stopped in the doorway and said, "Hello, Teri." It was Ed, the son-in-law of my boyfriend's godmother! We had gotten to know one another at family gatherings. This chance meeting blew my mind! Later, I thought, *The planets were aligned that day!* Sometimes, I think running into certain people in your life is meant to be.

The three of us chatted for another minute, and then the interview continued. As a result of running into Ed, I was surprisingly relaxed for the rest of the interview. Chuck asked me what my disability was. When I told him I had cerebral palsy, he told me his eight-year-old daughter had the same thing.

I was excited to learn about this connection. As it turned out, he told me toward the end of the interview, “One day I hope someone will give my daughter a chance with a job.” Instantly, I thought, *Maybe Chuck will understand and give me a job.*

A few days later, Chuck’s secretary called to tell me I was chosen for the position. I couldn’t believe my luck. When I hung up, I sobbed with joy and relief that I had been hired. My life was about to change, and this wasn’t lost on me.

A side note: Chuck retired in 2010 after a long career with BPA. His daughter, now with a master’s degree, still hadn’t found a job at that time. To this day, I wonder if anyone ever gave her a chance.

Proud to be Working

As a clerk typist in BPA’s Finance and Budget Office, I was ecstatic to finally have a real job. My main responsibility was to assist the manager’s secretary. At times, she was hard to deal with and if she was in a bad mood, she could be harsh. My duties included sorting and delivering mail, answering phones, typing memos, and filing. As time went on, it was evident to my co-workers that I had a brain.

In the beginning, I loved getting ready for work and going into the office. I felt like an adult with something to contribute. I was thrilled that my employers also gave me the opportunity to prove that I was smart enough and capable of learning new things. Finally, I was going to be defined by something other than how I physically came into the world. As time passed, I met people and became more comfortable with the work and the people.

When I first got my job, Matt was surprised, and he wasn't happy. He really didn't think anyone would hire me, plus he liked having me at home. It occurred to me that maybe he was scared I would be more independent.

A few months after I got the job, Matt and I had some friends over for dinner. While I was in the bathroom, I overheard him say how proud he was of me. "So many people can work, and they don't. Teri could stay home if she wanted to. It's not easy to get to work every day, but she does it."

When I heard that, it made me smile. I knew Matt was proud of me. It just took him some time to get used to me working.

Public Transportation

The weekend before I started work at BPA, I took a dry run on Portland's light rail, called MAX, so I'd know exactly how to get to my new job. I was worried about how long it would take me to walk from the MAX station to the BPA building. I timed myself because I did not want to be late, especially on my first day. On May 22, 1988, I started my first real job and took the next step in establishing a secure and independent life for myself.

I took public transportation to work every day, commuting from Gresham, a city just east of Portland, to Northeast Portland. It usually took me about 20 minutes from the MAX stop where Matt dropped me off, to reach my stop at the Lloyd Center stop. The BPA building was across the street. Back then, I didn't have a scooter yet, so I had to walk, using my walker, to get from the MAX stop to the BPA building, then up to my desk on the second floor. This short walk took me about 15 minutes and lots of energy—a walk that would take an able-bodied person about two minutes. It was tiring, and in the rain even worse, but I was determined to make it work.

Years later, a work friend told me he used to see me walking to BPA in those early days, and he had the urge to physically pick me up and carry me to the building. I laughed and told him, "I wish you would have!"

After a few months, BPA offered to provide an electric scooter so I could get around the building. It was amazing what a difference the scooter made. My lunch hour was no longer taken up just walking back and forth from the cafeteria. Simple things like a scooter are life-changing inventions for people with mobility challenges. With a scooter, the world opens up and daily life tasks become astonishingly easier—like a simple trip to a store.

Dressing for Work

Every night after work when I got home, I started preparing for the next workday. Once I got into some comfortable clothes, I'd start planning my clothes and shoes for the next day. I'd put them in the bathroom, take a shower, and eat dinner. I'd take care of my laundry, my other household responsibilities, and then head to bed. Ordinary preparations could easily take twice as long for me with my CP. If possible, I tried to fall asleep around 11:00 p.m. and usually got up around 5:30 a.m. to prepare for work.

On a good day, it took me about an hour to dress for work, including makeup and hair. To this day, the easiest place for me to get dressed and undressed is sitting on the toilet, which is just the right height with a solid seat. I can put my pants and shoes on without falling off the seat. I hated winter in Portland because it required more clothes. The fewer clothes, the better for me timewise. Often, I have wanted to live in a tropical climate where I only needed a bikini and shorts!

As time went by, I got a bit faster. A full make-up job has been important to me because I feel ugly all day if my make-up isn't stellar. For 24 years, this was my typical routine preparing for work each day. If I woke up late for work, it was a problem; I couldn't just jump into my clothes and rush out the door.

Once I was ready for work, then I had to ride my scooter to a MAX station and take light rail to work. This usually took another 30 minutes.

Obnoxious Comments

My new scooter at work inspired more obnoxious comments and behavior from co-workers. One day, I was in the elevator and this woman said to me, "Those scooters are so fun. My mom and I rent them at Disneyland all the time."

Ugh! People do not realize my scooter is not a toy to me and I'm not in it for the fun. A co-worker once said, "Sometimes, I envy you. I want a scooter." Immediately, I responded, "I'd trade you any day."

There was one IT guy at work who seemed a bit creepy to me. He regularly put his foot out as I was going by and he'd tell me to run over it with my scooter. He did this for the longest time, thinking he was funny. Finally, one day I got so irritated I ran over his foot! He looked at me in amazement, but he never did it again.

Another time, I was driving down the hall and the same smart ass stepped right in front of me. I stopped suddenly and the basket of my scooter was right at his crotch level. He just looked at me, smiling. I tried to go to the right, and he moved to the right. I turned to the left, and he moved to the left, hanging on to the basket each time. I tried to turn my scooter, but he kept blocking me. It was creepy because I was basically eye-level with his crotch during this power struggle. Finally, he let me go after he had his fun.

With 20/20 hindsight, I now see that my co-worker was a bully and that he was harassing me. Rarely did I do anything about those situations, other than respond with sarcasm. If I worried about everything that was said to me, I'd be filing harassment suits or suing people constantly.

I wish "constantfuckingly" was a word! I don't want to spend my life that way—it would make me bitter. Early along, I decided I'd rather be happy and have fun in my life. I'll usually stick up for myself in some way, hoping it will teach people something about respecting others—no matter what!

Moving on Up

A turning point early along at BPA was the day the secretary was out of the office. The boss was preparing for a business trip and needed his travel itinerary completed and submitted to management. In other words, lots of forms had to be completed and signed. Remember, it was the government! He handed me this pile of stuff. I told him I hadn't done a travel itinerary before. He said, "You'll learn."

After numerous questions on the telephone with another secretary, I successfully completed my boss's travel plans. When his secretary returned, she was surprised and congratulated me. After that, I realized I could accomplish whatever I was given. The secretary handed over timesheets for 30 employees for me to manage. Not a fun task because people complained about everything, but a job I could handle easily.

Two years later, I moved on to become a Procurement Clerk at BPA, then as secretary to the manager, Bob. He was my favorite boss in all my years at BPA. Not only because he was a smart, nice man, but he regularly told me I was smart, and he encouraged me to speak up in meetings and give my opinions. Repeatedly, he told me he valued what I thought. Bob also let me participate in prospective employee interviews, which was interesting. His opinion of me meant a lot. Bob would say, "You could run BPA." That always made me laugh yet also made me feel more confident.

Driving a Car

In my mid-20s, I decided to try driving a car. Someone must've told me I couldn't drive and of course, that pissed me off, so I set out on a quest to drive a car. Remember: Whenever people say I can't do something, then I'm determined to prove that I can do it.

To drive I had to first buy a car, install hand controls, have a brake put on the passenger side, and then find a driving instructor. Before I went through all that, I checked to see if I could just go to a driving school. When I researched this, I was told they had no cars equipped with hand controls. I had to ask, "Why? Do you think handicapped people don't drive?"

That's why I had to get a brake installed on the passenger side of my car. This was so I could take driving lessons. Nothing is ever easy. Literally, everything I do that involves physical mobility seems to require double the effort on my part.

I bought a 1984 Jeep Cherokee, white with gold pin-striping and gold wheels. I found a driving instructor, a retired state police officer. We drove once a week, on the weekends, all over Portland. My instructor and I became friends during our time together and he took

Teri in her Jeep.

me out to lunch after a driving lesson and told me about his marriage and how unhappy he was. Still, he was a good driving teacher, and I passed my driver's test on the second try.

After all that effort to learn to drive, I decided I didn't really like driving. It stressed me out. I'd have dreams of getting in bad car crashes. In my nightmares, my foot got stuck under the gas pedal and I'd struggle to manually pull my foot back from the pedal before crashing. There were a few times when my foot really did get stuck under the gas pedal.

For me, one car accident changed everything. Early one evening after work, I was driving on a one-way street in Portland, which is generally confusing for most drivers. This one-way street is shared with the light-rail train and that makes it even more confounding. I was driving down this street to meet a friend for dinner. A little boy started to dart out in front of my car with his bike. Luckily, his sister pulled him back. I quickly swerved to the left of the lane to avoid him and I over corrected. My Jeep hit the left curb, flew up in the air and landed, straddling the train tracks! It was like an episode from *Dukes of Hazard.* When my car landed on the tracks, my tires popped. Fortunately, no train was coming or I would've been dead.

After that accident, I became increasingly nervous about driving. Eventually, I sold my car and gave up driving after only five years. Honestly, driving was not something I felt comfortable with and enjoyed, but at least I proved I could drive.

Chapter 14
Movin' On

Matt got drunk on Olde English 800, regularly, and asked me to marry him a lot. At the time, a part of me wanted to because I was crazy in love with him, but I knew he really didn't want to get married because he'd been married twice and both wives had died. The first wife died from breast cancer after they divorced. His second wife died from a bad reaction to fertility drugs. She went into a coma and never recovered.

Beginning of the End

About two years after we had been together, Matt bought me a sapphire ring with small diamonds on each side set on a gold band that was dainty and twisted. He told me it was for my left hand, third finger. Then he added, "If I ever do get married, you'll be the one."

When I heard that, I thought, *I'm not so sure that's true, but it feels good to hear it.*

In 1989, Matt sold the house on Foster Road that he had bought years earlier with his second wife and then bought a house in Sandy, not far from where I spent my childhood. This move brought me much closer to Nana and Bapa's house, which was nice, but it got a lot harder for me to get to work in Northeast Portland. The commute was about 26 miles, and it took about one hour to get to work during traffic hours. Fortunately, for a few years I carpooled with another BPA employee who lived in Sandy, too, and we became friends.

Moving to Sandy was the beginning of the end of the Matt and Teri story. He started hanging out in his shop all the time, which was on his property. Even though Matt was home, I felt increasingly alone. He became more of a recluse. I couldn't get him to go anywhere—not even out to dinner. We grew apart emotionally, even though we still had sex all the time. His drinking now started before noon. His forgetfulness got worse, and he couldn't remember most things I told him. Constantly, I had to repeat myself. Matt got mad often and yelled and screamed at me. You could say the thrill was gone!

The Breakup

During the downward spiral of our relationship, I found out Matt was fucking around with a 20-year-old woman who worked up the street at a gas station/restaurant. A month later, I moved into an apartment in Gresham. The day I moved, Matt, my aunt, and my uncle helped me. It was the most emotional day of my life, and for the next two years my heart was broken.

Immediately, I got an extra job working at Nordstrom as a telephone operator on the weekends just to keep my mind off the breakup. From BPA, it was a couple blocks to Lloyd Center. So, when I got off work on Fridays at BPA, I'd go straight over to Nordstrom and work until closing. Saturdays, I went in about 10:00 a.m. and worked until 6:00 p.m. On Sundays, I only worked about four hours. I hated being in my apartment alone, and at 27 years old, this was the first time I had ever lived by myself.

To this day, I hate living alone. It's far too lonely for me and I get anxiety if I even think about it. I don't know if that makes me weak or not, but at least I admit it. Something I know about myself is that I need to be around people. When alone, I tend not to eat and I lose weight, which I can't really afford to do.

I had been working at Nordstrom a few months through the holidays. After December, Nordstrom management laid people off, but they wanted me to keep working for them. However, I didn't return to Nordstrom because my supervisor didn't put me back on the work schedule. It was odd and I couldn't figure out what was going on. Were they too scared to tell me they were laying me off? I never heard back again, so that job just became another odd work experience in my life. Fortunately, my regular full-time job at BPA continued.

After I had moved out, Matt came to my apartment occasionally. We'd have sex, drink, and talk. When I admit this, I fear I sound like such a loser, but at the time he was the love of my life. I couldn't help it. Matt told me he needed to decide what he wanted to do in his own life. A part of me hoped we'd get back together, and if he had asked, I would have. We had been together so long, I didn't want to throw it all away. He once told me, crying, "I love you so much, but it got harder for me to watch you every day. I wish I could give you my legs so you could walk."

When I heard that, I tried to lighten the moment because it crushed me. Jokingly, I said, "Your legs wouldn't match my body." Still, I felt crushed when I heard that was his reasoning for the split. Yet, I knew it was something I couldn't change.

"I love you, but I can't handle being with a crippled girl anymore because I want to fix you," Matt admitted while drunk. When he said that, I thought, *Here it is again, causing problems in my love life. It's always there, reminding me.*

At the time, I didn't believe Matt meant it in a bad way. He was just telling me, honestly, how he was feeling.

Still, it was excruciatingly hard to hear because I loved him. This broke my heart because there was nothing I could do about having CP. Matt said he'd love me forever, and I was the prettiest girl he was ever with. I guess that was supposed to make me feel better, but it didn't.

My reason for the breakup was his cheating and drinking!

Ever since hearing those words from Matt many years ago, I have worried. A part of me fears that even though I may be in a long-term relationship with someone, one day he'll suddenly realize I can't walk and dump me because he can no longer handle it. I couldn't help but think, *This is fucked news for me!*

It would be better if a man broke up with me because he thought I was a bitch rather than because he couldn't handle my CP. The reason I think like this is because everyone can be a bitch; but not everyone has physical handicaps. Everyone is crippled emotionally in some way—it's called, "No one is perfect."

For the record, I'm not a bitch. I do stick up for myself. If I didn't, I'd probably be curled up in the fetal position right now, stop writing, and never leave my house.

Lessons Learned

Alcoholism ran in Matt's family. He went to Vietnam right out of high school, ended up in jungle school and trained to be a paratrooper. I imagine he saw and did a lot of haunting things that he just couldn't shake. I'm sure the Vietnam War didn't help his drinking problem, along with having two wives who died. Years after we broke up, Matt did quit drinking, and he seems much happier now.

Matt taught me a lot about being in a relationship. I don't regret a minute of it because I have lots of good memories. Overall, he treated me good. We laughed a lot, and I think we both respected each other. If you really love someone, I don't believe you can hate them when it's over. I loved Matt, but I knew I had to move on. We eventually stopped hooking up with each other. It only happened occasionally for about a year, and we called one another every so often. In time, we faded from one another's life.

The Single Life

For the next couple of years, I mostly worked and hung out with friends. I had a few dates, but nothing earth shattering. This one guy, Kyle, had thick, brown, rock-star hair and stood over six-feet tall. He was cute and I liked him, but we were just fuck buddies. It lasted a few months and was fun, but nothing more. I couldn't help but compare everyone to Matt.

Then there was Sam, a guy I met at the health club where I swam regularly, a major form of exercise for me. I love swimming because I can walk in the pool. Sam was not my type, but he was nice, so I agreed to go on a date. Honestly, I can say it ended up officially being the most bizarre date I ever had, and I had some odd dates!

It began when we went to a drive-in. We went to see that dumb movie, *Werewolf,* with Jack Nicholson. Sam drove an old yellow truck with a bench seat, so I sat next to him, and he put my walker in the truck bed. He bought all my favorite candy—Butterfingers, Milk Duds, Red Vines—and we settled in to watch the movie. About 10 minutes into it, my door flew open and a dark-haired girl with glasses began shrieking at the top of her lungs: "You fucking asshole! Who the fuck is she? I hate you!"

She went on and on, swearing at Sam. I was frozen in my seat, looking at her as she screamed. Worried, I thought, *She might pull me from the truck and beat me up.*

Sam quickly got out and met her at the back of the truck. By this time, I was crouched down in the seat, hoping not to get killed, wishing I was home in bed.

While they were screaming at the back of the truck, I heard her say, "What's that?"

Sam said, "It's her walker."

Then she said, "Oh, ok, whatever, if that's what you want!"

When I heard that, I wanted to raise my head from the backseat and yell, "Hey, fuck you!"

Instead, I decided to keep my mouth shut. Honestly, I felt incredibly vulnerable and scared for my physical safety, not knowing what this crazy girl was going to do. After that scene ended, Sam asked if I wanted to go home. Without a second's hesitation, I said, "Yes!"

The next day Sam sent me a dozen roses at work. My boss said with a smile, "Wedding bells, I hear?"

I said, "I don't hear anything!"

After that, Sam's ex broke into his phone and heard my message thanking him for those flowers. Oops! He took her to the hospital that night. She had tried to kill herself.

Sam asked me out a few more times, but I thought it would be against my better judgment. Later, Sam told me he moved back in with his mom to get away from this woman because "she was like a stalker." In the end, he married her!

Chapter 15
Love and Marriage

In 1994, my old roommate and best friend, Kelly, was back in town. We hadn't seen each other in five years. After college, she worked as a nanny in Germany and then returned to Portland. The first time we got together, we went to a Fourth of July party at her friend's house. When we got there, I realized I didn't know anyone. Kelly soon changed that situation. On her way to the bathroom, she looked across the backyard and saw a guy she used to work with. Kelly turned to me and said, "That's Joel Siri. I used to work with him. You two will get along great; you both like to swear!"

Kelly quickly introduced us and then headed to the bathroom. Joel ended up hanging out with us most of the evening. When he asked how old I was and I told him 29, he said, "You are well preserved."

This made me laugh, especially at my ripe old age. "I'm not 90!"

The Girl on the Scooter

After that party, I didn't expect to see Joel again, but a few days later he showed up at my work with a dozen bagels. He worked at his cousin's bagel shop in Northeast Portland, about 10 minutes from my work. When Joel asked for me at BPA's reception desk, he only knew my first name, so he described me to the security guard: "She has a scooter and long brown hair."

This was not a common description for BPA employees. Most people there referred to me as "the girl on the scooter." If they didn't know my name, everyone knew me by that description. The security guard called and said, "There's a guy in the lobby with bagels."

I knew who it was, so I quickly put on red lipstick and went out to the lobby. He gave me fresh warm bagels to share with my co-workers. It was a kind and friendly gesture, and I thought, *He is cute and normal, and he doesn't seem to have any weird baggage like ex-girlfriends stalking him.*

My co-workers became instant fans of Joel because of the bagels.

He hung out for a bit, and we chatted in the lobby. Out of the corner of my eye, I noticed co-workers conveniently walking by, checking him out, saying, "Hey Teri." Obviously, they were curious about the bagel boy.

Joel was a huge improvement compared to the other guys I had been meeting. He awkwardly suggested that we should go out for drinks with Kelly. I told him that would be a blast. Later, when I mentioned this to Kelly, she refused to go, saying, "He really doesn't want to go for drinks with me, it's you he wants to have drinks with!"

First Date with Joel

A few days later, Joel and I met at a Thai restaurant I had recommended. It was his first time eating Thai food, so I ordered for us. As I dished up the food, I was nervous and spilled a big blob on the table. I apologized and Joel just laughed; he didn't think it was a big deal. Dinner conversation was fun with lots of laughing. We conversed like we had known each other for a while; we were easy friends from the beginning.

After dinner, Joel suggested a coffee house in the neighborhood. It sounded like a good idea to me, but I soon realized he didn't have a car—he had a bicycle.

Instantly, I was stressed out because I was going to have to walk about four blocks. I thought, *Oh my god, ok, I'll just do it because I don't want to seem crippled!*

As we walked, Joel didn't seem at all concerned that it took me maybe an hour to walk four blocks—or maybe it was a mile? All I know is it was a long fucking walk. By the time we got there, I was so unbelievably tired, and my arms were numb, I thought if I had to lift my walker down one more curb, I was going to drop it and fall on my face. While I was plodding down the street, I thought, *All of this hassle and pain just to seem normal, and on top of that, I don't even drink coffee!*

By the time we got to the coffee shop, I couldn't feel my hands holding on to the walker handles. I was sweaty, I had cottonmouth, and I was convinced I had lost five pounds on that walk. Even my new shoes got holes in the soles! But I had fun, and in a way, I liked that Joel was oblivious to my "cerebral palsy-ness." My longing to be seen and treated like a normal person superseded all the pain and exhaustion of the evening stroll to get coffee.

Family Emergency

Joel asked me out for a second date, but I couldn't go due to a medical emergency in my family. My mom had a brain aneurysm, and my family went into panic mode. Tami flew to Portland from San Diego and Traci came from Lake Tahoe. We spent five days at the hospital holding vigil for Mom, who had brain surgery. I had been at the hospital for a couple days and made a quick trip home to shower and call Joel to tell him what was going on. I hoped he believed me because it sounded like such a dramatic excuse, but then again, it's not like I said I had to wash my hair. Besides, I thought, *What decent human being would say her mom had brain surgery just to get out of a date?*

A few days later, Kelly showed up at the hospital with Joel. I was upset, not mad, but shocked because I had no makeup on and I had been in the same clothes for a couple of days. I was still super self-conscious about how I looked. Joel didn't care that I didn't have makeup on, but I did. "Kelly, I can't believe you brought him!" I did think it was sweet, I was just caught off guard.

Kelly responded, "Joel wanted to come. He just wanted to see you."

My fear of not being put together when in public has always been the case with me, even to this day. I don't feel good about myself in public without makeup, especially with people I don't know. Makeup and nice clothes help my self-confidence.

Nana and Bapa, along with my aunts and cousins, were at the hospital, too. Everyone got an introduction to Joel much sooner than I had planned. Joel's introduction to my mom was in her hospital room with half her head shaved and one eye swollen shut. She was sitting up in bed and waved to Joel, cheerfully telling him he looked like Mel Gibson! I thought to myself, *Those are some good drugs Mom is taking!*

When Joel and Kelly left the hospital, I walked them out. I heard everyone whispering behind us. "Oh, aren't they cute together!" Embarrassed, I turned and looked at them, as if to say, "We can hear you. Shut up!" Later, Nana told me she liked Joel's laugh, and other family members had good things to say, too.

Marriage, Seriously?

Eventually, Mom got out of the hospital and fully recovered. Joel and I had many dates, and we didn't have sex until we had been dating for three months. That was highly unusual. At first, I thought he just wanted to be friends since we waited awhile before having sex. My relationship with Matt was the exact opposite. Joel's libido was definitely different than Matt's. It took some adjusting since I liked sex more often. Four or five times a week was fine with me because sex makes me feel close to my partner. When we first started sleeping together, Joel and I might have had sex twice a week. For a new relationship, that was different for me. I also thought it would change, reassuring myself, *He must just be shy.*

Later, I learned that it was just the way Joel was.

In time, I also learned that as an artist, Joel placed his art above all else. He painted in acrylics, oil, and watercolors, and at the time, he painted every day. His art is what really brings him the most happiness.

A little less than a year into our relationship, Joel asked me to marry him in a very odd way—but memorable. He was housesitting for his cousin and invited me over for dinner. While he prepared dinner, I told him my mom had been living in my apartment for about a year, and it was starting to get on my nerves. "I am going to start looking for another apartment," I declared.

With his head in the refrigerator, looking for something, Joel nonchalantly replied, "We should just get married."

I laughed and said, "Yeah, sure, that'd be fun."

Nothing more was discussed. A couple days later, I went to his cousin's home again for dinner. Joel and I were just chatting about our day when he said, "I was telling some of my friends about our plans."

I turned to him with a quizzical look on my face and asked, "What plans?"

"You know, getting married."

Speechless, I didn't say anything. I had no idea Joel was serious. Finally, I said just that! "Are you serious?"

My mind was racing: How was I supposed to know that was a serious proposal? I never thought I'd get married and if I did, I had hoped it'd be a little more romantic.

When I shared some of my thoughts with Joel, again, he asked me to marry him. This time I said, "Yes."

I decided, *Joel is a super nice guy and I think he'd be a good man to settle down with. Besides, we both like a lot of the same things.*

Tying the Knot

We didn't get married until a year later. Mom moved out of my apartment and Joel moved in. Honestly, I was hesitant about relationships after Matt, half expecting Joel to break up with me because it was too hard being with me—even though he loved me. Breaking up is difficult for me, and the thought of divorce was even worse, so we waited almost a year to get married.

On my grandparents' anniversary, March 12, we got hitched at the Multnomah County courthouse. I wore a long red dress, and Joel wore black pants and a denim, button-down shirt with a black vest. Our ceremony was casual, low key, and took about 10 minutes. The jury box in the courtroom was filled with mostly my family from out of town. My sisters, parents, my dad's wife, aunts and uncles, and cousins Jeff and Rodney, along with all their significant others. Of course, Nana and Bapa were there, and they signed the marriage certificate as our witnesses. Joel's mom, dad, and grandpa were there, too, along with a couple of his long-time friends.

We had a reception at Cassidy's in downtown Portland. As a gift, Kelly hired a professional photographer, and we had unique, black and white photos taken. My friend Lisa brought a money tree to the reception, which helped pay for the honeymoon. Some of my co-workers

Teri and Joel's wedding day, 1996.

came to the reception and one of Joel's brothers joined us along with two of his cousins. So many people bought me drinks at the reception, but I was only able to sip on one all day!

Some of Joel's family members were bothered because we didn't send out invitations. My perspective was, "It's a Tuesday at the courthouse, I don't think that warrants invitations."

A big wedding didn't interest us, hence, the courthouse. It's just how we chose to do it. We decided to spend most of our money on the honeymoon—not a big wedding.

After the reception, we spent the night at a popular destination not far from Portland called McMenamin's Edgefield. By the time we got there, my feet hurt so badly and we were so tired, we just stayed in our room. Joel bought food at the pub, and we ate dinner on the bed in our room while we counted wedding cash!

European Honeymoon

About three weeks after our wedding, we went on an unforgettable honeymoon. We flew to Rome and stayed at a five-star hotel; unlike anything I had ever experienced. It had high ceilings with big columns, and a sizable gray-and-pink marbled bathroom with a heated towel rack. The balcony looked over the Via Veneto, one of the most elegant, expensive streets in Rome. I had no idea we were staying in such a swanky place since we had left all the planning up to our travel agent. She did not disappoint.

Rome was the home of the best carbonara pasta I had ever tasted. To this day, I still think about that Italian dish. Some of the restaurants where we ate had doorways that were too narrow for my wheelchair, so waiters came outside, picked me up, and carried me through the door. I loved it—and I couldn't help but take note that all those Italian men were hot!

We visited the Trevi Fountain, one of the most famous fountains in the world, and threw coins and made wishes. We saw the Pantheon of Rome, and Joel walked the Spanish steps—all 135 of them—while I watched. Some nights, we just strolled through the city's narrow streets. Actually, I rolled with my chair and Joel walked. The streets of Rome were interesting because one side would have a curb cut with a blue handicapped sign, indicating to people like me to cross at that spot; but directly across the street the curb was high, at least 10 inches, without a curb cut. So, we would pop a wheelie every time we had to cross to the other side of the street. I found the thinking behind the curb situation comical.

On the third day, we boarded the cruise ship *Renaissance* in Rome and set sail for Greece. The ship was small but classy and only held 114 people, including the crew. The rooms were appointed with elegant teak paneling and mirrors. By far, this was the most high-class vacation this girl had ever been on.

As we crossed the Ionian Sea between Italy and Greece, I got the worst case of seasickness, ever. I kept thinking, *What a great way to spend a honeymoon—puking my guts out.*

The ship's doctor came to our room, took one look at me, and said, "Oh, my!" He gave me a shot for the nausea and vomiting, explaining this particular shot was "legal in international waters." I didn't know what it was, but it worked; well, at least I was able to stop puking. This severe case of seasickness had broken all the capillaries in my face, and I had little red dots all over. I looked horrible.

Determined, Despite Obstacles

When I awoke the next morning, we were at port in Greece. The ship's crew was concerned I wouldn't be able to make the shore excursion up to the Oracle of Delphi. They advised us against going, but I was determined to go. So, Joel and I, along with two guys who helped us, were the first people to reach the Oracle. There were marble steps going all the way up the hill that led to Delphi. One man got on my left and the other on my right, and they picked up the sides of my wheelchair and up we went.

It was beautiful to see a place I had read about in history books. The Delphi had been built along a mountainside and because it was springtime, the whole mountain was blanketed in bright yellow flowers with the backdrop of a bright, cloudless blue sky. I was so happy with myself that I had persevered and pursued a travel experience I hoped for, despite the discouraging people and physical obstacles. My independence and determination served me well on that honeymoon trip.

The cruise included going through the Corinth Canal that connects The Gulf of Corinth to the Aegean Sea. It was so narrow, only 75-feet wide; I could almost touch the walls of the canal, and I could read the carvings on the walls perfectly as our small cruise ship moved through.

On the ship, I used my walker mostly. My wheelchair was reserved for outings that required a lot of walking or keeping up with a tour group. I preferred my walker because it was easier to use.

Throughout most of the trip, Joel and I frequently heard, "She probably won't be able to do this, or that." Fill in the blanks. I got so tired of people telling me what I wasn't going to be able to do. Instead, I did just about everything with few exceptions. However, I did not make it up to the Parthenon temple at the Acropolis, but Joel went to the top while I waited at the bottom in my wheelchair. Later, we had drinks in a bar a few miles away with a perfect view of the Acropolis. Joel told me all about his walk to the top. As we talked, I gazed out the window in disbelief that I was there, thrilled to be in the presence of Athen's historic Acropolis.

Chapter 16
Joy and Grief

In the beginning, our marriage was good, and I loved being married. I wanted one of those marriages that lasted 50 years. Joel and I were good friends, and we liked being together. A year before we got married, we had bought a house together, so we spent lots of time creating a home. The only tough part about being together was Joel starting a new job and soon quitting, trying to find his place in the workforce. He went through a lot of jobs.

Socially, we had lots of fun and did many things together. We went to movies, dinner, out for drinks, and travelled often. Joel didn't treat me differently because I had CP. He did the household chores and cooking. He is a natural clean freak and loves to cook, so housework was no big deal. Besides, Joel was a much better cook than me. I cooked occasionally when I had days off. It took me hours to prepare meals, so I didn't cook on a weeknight. I can make great chocolate chip cookies, but even that is an all-day undertaking that I reserved for the weekend.

Smart, Conscientious, Detail Oriented

Life was humming along. My marriage was in a good place and my work was mostly satisfactory. My biggest career change happened when I got a job as a scheduler, buying and selling electric power hourly in

Nana and Teri, 2004.

what is called “real time.” This job is similar, in ways, to working on the stock market, but selling power for BPA. When I first applied for the job, I overheard Bob’s glowing recommendation of me to my future boss. He said, “She is smart, conscientious, and detail oriented.” At the end of the conversation, Bob added, “Teri is like a ray of sunshine in the corner.”

After that, I got an interview. This was the one and only time in my life I knew before the interview was over that I had the job in the bag. My new boss told me during the interview that I had the best recommendation he’s ever gotten about anyone. There were three people in that interview, and we were yacking like we knew each other for years.

Scheduler was a hard, high-pressure job, at times. I worked 12-hour, rotating shifts for three years, including some weekends. My confidence grew because the feedback from managers and co-workers was positive, and they thought highly of my abilities. Many times on stressful, busy days when power lines were down, energy got cut hourly, and phones rang nonstop for 10 hours, co-workers said they wanted to work with me because I did a good job and made them laugh.

In time, BPA gave me formal recognition and awards for my expertise as a scheduler. I was told in a performance review that I was among the top three schedulers. Full of confidence, I finally felt like I knew what I was doing and was valued. In turn, I got to train new people.

What's Wrong with You?

In general, life was good, but there was the regular onslaught of people making rude and oblivious statements about my CP. It's as if my personhood was always secondary to my CP. One time at a BPA party with some of my co-workers and their spouses, I met an incredibly rude man who was a co-worker's husband. He came up to me, looked me up and down as I was standing with my walker, next to Joel, then asked, "What's your affliction?"

At first, I didn't know what he was talking about. I looked at my zipper, thinking it might be down. I was taken aback because he didn't even bother to introduce himself. This happens a lot. People ask me what's wrong with me physically, even before asking my name! The rude man then looked at Joel and started asking Joel about his work, as if Joel worked at BPA. His wife interrupted, saying, "Teri works with me, not Joel."

Her husband looked genuinely surprised. I felt like sarcastically saying, "I know, can you believe it?" Instead, I said nothing but thought plenty. Most of my thoughts had lots of bleeps, but I was at a work function, so I chose to bite my tongue. But I wanted to say, "Fuck you, dummy. Yes! I have a better job than you!"

Nosey Strangers

When I got married, I knew it would open a whole new can of worms—I mean questions—from all kinds of nosey people, many I didn't even know! The comments were constant. Some were just downright hurtful, although I don't think they were meant to be.

People would see my wedding ring and ask, somewhat shocked, "Oh, you're married?" When I'd hear that question, I often thought, *You might as well say, "Who would marry you."*

The next question would then be, "Is your husband handicapped, too?" To this unbelievable question I'd answer sarcastically, "Not physically."

When someone I don't know asks that question, I feel as if there is this unspoken rule that I'm not allowed to marry outside "my people." To assume I'd only be married to another crippled guy is one more wonky stereotype about people with disabilities. They might as well be saying to a married Black woman, "Is your husband Black, too?"

Once nosey strangers realized I wasn't married to someone with a physical disability, then they'd say something like, "It takes a really nice guy to be with someone like you, I bet."

Hard to believe, but I got that comment a lot. Sometimes, when my patience was low, I'd respond, "No, my husband can be an asshole just like everyone else's." In truth, no one would ever describe Joel as an asshole.

Luckily, I have a sense of humor, but I realized long ago that I gotta laugh at these intrusive questions and statements, even when deep down this stuff just chips away at my soul—and I feel exhausted.

Can You Have Children?

Not long after we got married, people frequently asked if I was going to have children. Or a more invasive question, "Can you have kids?"

The answer I gave when asked was, "No." And when they asked, "Can you?" I'd say, "Yes." I did not provide any further explanation but just kept them hanging.

In truth, I never had a burning desire to be a mom. I just figured the world already had plenty of children, it didn't need mine. Instead, I wanted to travel and lead an exciting life. I did not want to be tied down and worrying about children for the rest of my life. I believe you have to be willing to put in the time when raising a child to end up with a decent, happy, well-adjusted adult. I wasn't willing to do that. When I did share my feelings about kids, many people told me that I was selfish.

Honestly, I just wasn't willing to go through the hassles of trying to take care of a baby and rearing a child when I already struggled with having CP. Just taking care of myself was a big job. In the end, it boiled down to being scared. No offense to those who have kids and are handicapped. I admire their love and commitment to having a family, but I had to be honest with myself and admit that wasn't me. I am perfectly content being the favorite aunt.

My good friend Lisa, who has CP, birthed and raised two kids along with her husband. Their children are grown now, and Lisa and Steve clearly did a great job. After almost 20 years of not saying anything about my decision to be childless, Lisa admitted to me that she was pissed off at me some 30 years earlier when I told her the reasons I didn't want kids. At the time, I told Lisa, "It's great for you—not me. We are two totally different people. My reasons for not having kids have nothing to do with your choice to have kids."

Once we talked about it more, Lisa understood my feelings better. Initially, she felt like it was a slam against her. That could not have been further from the truth. She did a great job as a mother, but I felt as though I

Teri's niece and nephew, Alix and Aaron.

may not have that kind of strength and determination to raise a child.

On the other hand, there were many people in my life who, without my even asking, told me, "You have no business having kids."

Whenever I heard that statement, that's when I wanted to have several children because they somehow thought they had the right to dictate "do's and don'ts" to me. As I've said, when someone tells me I can't do something, that's when I go ahead and do that very thing. Ultimately, having a child was a little far to go to prove a point!

But I do love being an aunt! Traci loves her kids more than anyone or anything in the world, and I am right behind her, loving my twin's kids! Her children, Aaron and Alix, are great, inside and out. If I had kids, I'd want them to be just like Traci's. I love my niece and nephew as if they were my own. Traci has done a great job showering them with love, and as their aunt, I just add to the love fest.

Is She Your Sister?

One time, Joel's co-worker Pat came over to our house because he wanted Joel to do a drawing for him. When I got home that day, I drove my scooter into the garage like I did every day and used my walker to go into the house through the garage. Joel and Pat were talking in the kitchen and saw me come in. Pat was an older, grey-haired, heavyset man. When he first saw me, his mouth literally fell open. Now, I'd like to say it was because of my beauty, but really it was because I was using a walker. He looked me up and down, and turned to Joel and asked, "Does she need any help? Is she ok?"

He asked Joel these questions while I stood right there, completely ignoring me, or my ability to speak for myself. People have done this a lot, as if my difficulty walking means I can't hear them—or I can't speak for myself.

Joel told him, "She's fine, she doesn't need help."

I introduced myself as Joel's wife and sat down. Then Pat turned toward Joel and continued to talk to him as if I wasn't there. He became one more person who launched into how "it takes a special guy to be with a girl like me."

Whenever I hear this kind of statement, I know they mean well, but it makes me feel like I am less of a woman. It sounds as if Joel did me a big favor by marrying me! Regularly, people who saw Joel and me together used to ask my husband, "Is she your sister?"

Joel would respond, "I don't kiss my sister."

Grief

A few months after Nana died in 2005, I decided to take a road trip and get away. After Nana's death, I was gripped with the worst grief I have ever felt. She was my best friend, and I had been consumed with acting as her conservator/guardian for the last three years of her life while I was working full time at BPA. I had promised Bapa that I would look out for Nana after he died in 1998. Nana moved back to the house she had built in the 1950s and was able to live independently with ongoing help from my Aunt Carol and Uncle Gary, Joel, me, and home caregivers. We wanted Nana to be comfortable in her own home for as long as possible. Only during the last weeks of her life did we have to move her to a nursing home due to a serious stroke.

After Nana died, Joel and I traveled through the Southwest for two weeks. We explored Zion National Park, Bryce Canyon National Park, and Red Rock Canyon. We camped the whole way and every day was spontaneous.

On our way to the Grand Canyon, we stopped at Lake Powell, one of my favorite places with its brilliant blue water, smooth as glass. I imagined walking on that lake, effortlessly. We slept in the back of our new green Honda Element with the hatch open, staring out on Lake Powell in the moonlight. The next morning, we woke up early and went swimming at the resort pool because the temperature was already in the 80s. At times like that, it feels so great to be alive.

On our trip home, we drove up the coast of California and Oregon on Highway 1. Our time on the road was exhilarating and freeing for me because I didn't have to plan a thing. My grief lightened a bit after that trip, but I would learn over the years that the ache in my heart for Nana is permanent and I think of her and talk to her every day. Until my last breath, I know Nana will be with me.

Chapter 17
When Love Fades

Over the years, I increasingly felt like I was married more to my best friend or caregiver, rather than a husband and lover. We had a great marriage in many ways, but I also wanted to come home from work and feel like my husband wanted me sexually. I like sex but I don't like to initiate everything all the time—and then get turned down. Too many times I felt vulnerable and rejected.

Monotony & Insecurity

The sexual rejection started doing crazy things to my head. I started to feel ugly, disgusting, and unwanted. Granted, I already felt self-conscious about my physical attractiveness. Sexual rejection made it worse. For a long time, I tried talking about this problem and asked Joel if there was something wrong. His usual response was, "I love you more than anything."

The way Joel showed his love in our marriage was by doing things for me. This was great but I needed someone who was excited to see me. Honestly, I wanted to have fun in bed, and I didn't feel I interested him in that way anymore.

Eventually, our marriage got monotonous. It seemed like Joel came home from work every night in a bad mood. After dinner, he'd watch TV and fall asleep. In turn, I became lonelier and more depressed. I started to think, *I should be happy just getting what I get, when I get it, and be happy because I am lucky someone married me!*

One night when we were in bed, I asked him why he didn't ever feel like having sex with me. I just wanted him to tell me if there was a problem. Joel was not a big talker about his feelings, but he got irritated with my questions and blurted out, "You don't arouse me."

That made me cry. After that night, Joel told me many times that he was just upset when he made that comment and he didn't really mean it. At the time, I just couldn't forget it, and even though Joel tried to reassure me that he didn't really mean it, the hurt and doubt went to the heart of my physical insecurities.

Divorce

This huge problem of not enough sexual intimacy finally caused me to ask for a divorce. To some, this might sound minor since everything else was great and he's a great guy, but for me it was not enough, striking at my deepest insecurities about my body. Over the years in my marriage, I kept feeling more unwanted.

When I told friends and co-workers I was getting divorced, almost all of them said, "Teri, are you sure you want to do that? He takes good care of you. How will you manage?" I thought to myself, *I took care of him, too.*

I understood their concerns, I had already thought of everything. Daily life would be a much bigger struggle than it already was, but it wouldn't be fair for me, or Joel, if I stayed just because I needed him to help me with the chores. Daily challenges were getting hard to deal with and I was getting older. Believe me, I just wanted to be happy and fulfilled like everyone else, but to feel whole again, I knew I had to make some big changes. Life is so short and whizzing by, so I knew

I had to stay honest with myself even though I had plenty of people telling me, "Stay."

Joel and I were together for 18 years and married for 16 of those years. Toward the end of our marriage, despite being best friends and doing everything together, I felt like I didn't really know him. The reason I say this is because when we discussed things, I usually felt like he told me what he thought I wanted to hear. Instead, I wanted to hear what he *really* thought.

In addition, he left most of the decision making in our relationship to me. I didn't want to be responsible for all the decisions. Sometimes, I wanted Joel to make decisions without asking me. Of course, there were things I needed to know when it came to major decisions, but I didn't want to decide everything, even down to dinner and movies. Joel would ask, "What do you want to do? Where do you want to go?"

I would say, "It's not always about me. What do you want?"

Longing for Partnership

At some point, I began to see how Joel gave up on a part of himself and his own desires because he was trying to be nice all the time and defer to whatever I wanted. What I wanted was a partnership in our marriage, more of a give and take, whether deciding how to spend the evening or making love. Along the way, Joel gave up hobbies and activities he liked. For starters, he liked to hike, bike, and do lots of outdoorsy things. When we got together, he stopped those activities. I would tell him, "Do what you want! If you want to go for a hike, then go do that."

He'd say, "I want you to come, I feel bad you can't hike with me."

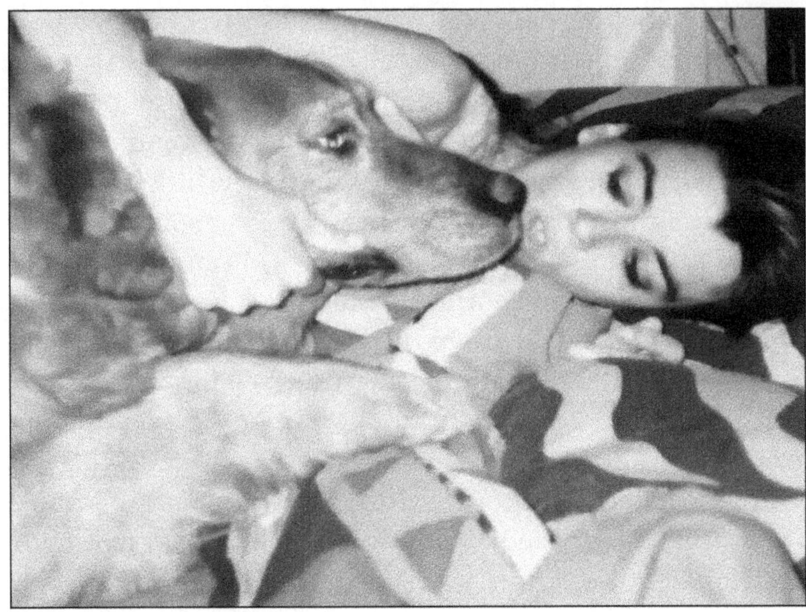

Teri snuggling with Gretzky.

Trying to be funny, I'd respond, "I'm the wrong girl for that." Then I'd add, "Don't feel bad. Those are things you like. Don't give them up because of me. Do them and tell me about it. There are plenty of other things we can do together."

During our marriage, we traveled a lot internationally and we saw many great places together. Travelling was my favorite thing to do with Joel.

Telling Joel I wanted a divorce was by far the hardest thing I've ever done in my life. I know I broke his heart. Mine was broken, too. When I got married, my hope was to have one of those 50-year marriages and still love each other in the end. I wanted to be like Nana and Bapa.

Many different feelings, including depression and anxiety, hung over me in the final years of our marriage. Honestly, I felt like I was bringing Joel down and I didn't want to do that. I also wanted to be happy, and I wanted Joel to be happy. So, I rolled the dice.

On My Own Again

Little Hoss and Teri.

Before our divorce was finalized, Joel moved out and I was living on my own again for the first time in almost 20 years. The loneliness was overwhelming, and I felt alone in the world, even though I had friends and family around me. Sometimes, it was so quiet in my small apartment all I heard was the refrigerator running. When my phone rang, it startled me, and I'd jump. I found myself looking forward to trips because it meant I got out and spent time with people who love me; but then, I had to come back to an empty apartment. I kept telling myself, *It's temporary. You can get through this one day at a time.*

The scary part was considering that this aloneness might become permanent. I would obsess over my aloneness: What if this becomes my life where I do most things alone? Go to the movies alone? Eat out alone? Go to the store alone? What if I'm all alone for the rest of my life?

On top of taking care of my personal needs, I also had to take care of my dog, Hoss, a stubborn little Pekingese. Joel and I had gotten our dog a few years after we were married as a companion for our older golden retriever, Gretzky. When we divorced, Joel didn't take Hoss because he was living at his mom's house. In the morning before leaving for work, I'd let

Hoss out to go to the bathroom and feed him. He was home alone all day in the kitchen, so as he got older, he had accidents in the house. Usually when I got home from work, I had a mess to clean up. It could take up to an hour, depending on where the accident was. It's hard for me to bend down, so I worried about falling because I can't get up on my own, depending on the way I fall. It's not pretty!

Hoss didn't listen to me like he did Joel. If he wanted out at night, I had to get up, let Hoss outside, and by then, I was wide awake, so I had trouble getting back to sleep. Once I was awake, my mind started racing—worrying about work, selling the house, my new life alone, and wondering what the future held for me. By the time I got back to sleep, the alarm went off and I had to start all over again.

Sometimes, it was all I could do to get myself something to eat. I didn't buy a lot of groceries because the food usually went bad and I ended up throwing most of it away. Besides, it wasn't fun cooking for one. It took a long time to prepare the food and a lot of effort, and in the end, I was eating alone. My only hope was to dive into the loneliness, be with it, and hope I'd find love again.

Our divorce was finalized in February 2012. Unquestionably, I missed the comfortable feeling that came with being in a long-term relationship.

Chapter 18
The Unraveling of My Work Life

After three years as a scheduler, I thought it was time for a change, inspired by a new year and a new millennium. I transferred to a job in our billing office, which handled billing for the power BPA bought and sold on real-time and on customer contracts.

In the beginning, I was confident in my abilities. However, billing office management changed several times, and the new managers did not seem as supportive or as fair as my managers in prior positions. As time went on, it became clear it wasn't my imagination. At the very least, I felt like I was not in the "preferred" crowd.

In billing, I rarely heard about the good job I did. Usually, I only heard about problems or issues. Initially, my job provided me with loads of confidence, but later it sapped my confidence. In turn, I became anxious, nervous, and physically sick.

Slipping Confidence

During the last six years of my career at BPA, I realized I had become more introverted. People even used the word introvert when describing me. In the past, that word was not used to describe me. With time, I began to doubt myself more and I lost even more self-confidence.

My problems at work began around 2006 when I applied for a higher-grade job as a Senior Revenue

Analyst. The job seemed more challenging and paid more. I didn't really want the new position as a senior analyst, but I applied because I thought the extra money would be helpful. Besides, only one other person was applying, and I thought I had a good chance of getting the position.

The supervisor who ended up hiring me for this job was not especially friendly toward me and I felt she didn't like me. I had known her since my days in procurement. When she told me I was hired, it wasn't a ringing endorsement of the faith she had in my ability to do the job. Instead, it felt more like, "Oh well, you're the only choice."

Usually when I was hired for a new position at BPA, the person hiring seemed happy to have me. In this case, I didn't feel that enthusiasm. Instead, it left me feeling paranoid, wondering, *Am I doing my job well enough?*

Pay Inequity

I was a Senior Revenue Analyst just shy of two years and doing extra duties with none of the pay that came with a GS-13 pay grade. This inequity completely stressed me out; promoted to the higher pay grade but not getting the increased pay. Others who became Senior Revenue Analysts told me they were given additional duties a little at a time. In my case, my boss handed me responsibilities immediately and I was expected to jump right in. My performance reviews were great, and co-workers offered positive feedback, along with people I worked with outside of the billing group. So, I didn't understand why I didn't get the pay raise along with my promotion. Statistically, people with physical disabilities are underpaid by 30 percent or more compared to able-bodied workers, all things being equal. At the time, I knew in my gut I was not being treated fairly and paid less than my co-workers.

During my performance review, when I asked about the pay increase that was supposed to go with the promotion, my supervisor said, "You are this close," as she held her index finger and thumb close together. I wondered, *Does that mean a few days, weeks, or months?*

I asked but wasn't told. There was a carrot on a stick that I could never quite reach. My boss also said she didn't feel like I had confidence, building a weak case against my competence. When she told me that, I thought, *Well, not giving me a pay promotion due me after almost two years, would make anyone feel unsure of themselves.*

The stress combined with a nagging feeling of being undervalued, wore on me and I started getting sick in the morning before work. I ended up requesting a return to my original job as a Revenue Analyst, since it didn't look like I was getting the bump in pay any time soon—and maybe never. Later, I learned co-workers who worked as Senior Revenue Analysts had all gotten their promotions in a matter of months. Not me. The more I learned from my co-workers, the more I had to consider that maybe my supervisor was biased against me and my abilities—or my physical disabilities.

If my supervisor didn't give me the promotion because of my performance, I should have received an unsatisfactory performance review, which I never got in the 24 plus years I worked at BPA. I was a team player and quickly stepped up to help co-workers regularly, if they asked. They thanked me and told me how approachable I was when they needed help.

When I returned to my previous duties, I thought things would improve, but I was still getting sick in the morning before work. On top of that, I started to get insomnia and began taking medicine for anxiety and depression. Instead of feeling more confident in a job I had spent 12 years doing, I felt less confident. A certain co-worker would ask me questions and then roll her eyes when I answered. That did a number on my head, too. I started to worry, *She thinks I'm stupid.*

My supervisor's disrespect began to collide with my slipping self-confidence. I started personal counseling to figure out why I let people get to me—especially at work. In other areas of my life, I thought I didn't care what people thought of me. After several months of counseling, I realized that maybe this was not really the case all the time. The clusterfuck of the fake promotion to Senior Revenue Analyst and my supervisor's attitude toward me were the real issues, and the stark truth of knowing I wasn't treated fairly.

Burn Out & Anxiety

Toward the end of my career at BPA, I got to work later every day. It became much harder after my divorce and living on my own, in addition to the reality of just being older and having less energy. I started taking Ambien to sleep and Celexa for anxiety and depression. I had been at this rigorous routine for 24 years and burn out was staring me in the face.

I started thinking about possibly retiring about a year before I took action. My depression, increasing anxiety, and looming divorce took a toll on me. Things were becoming harder to do, especially on my own. It was scary to think about retiring because I had been independent and had made my own money for years. I worried, *Will I have enough money?*

When I went to my doctor, she was surprised that I had lasted at my job as long as I had. She suggested early retirement, based on my declining health, both physically and mentally. I had another eight years at BPA before I could retire with company benefits. Although I had been told for years that I was strong, I started to worry about myself, feeling weak and vulnerable. A part of me felt like I was giving up on the very thing I tried to prove all my life—that I can do it!

Despite those feelings, I honestly felt like I would die prematurely if I continued dragging myself to an unhappy work situation. When I worried or got nervous about work, I'd get dry heaves, and I'd stop eating. Not good, especially for someone like me.

Disability Retirement

After consulting with my doctor, I started looking into applying for disability retirement and figure out what I needed to do to get the process started. I found a Portland attorney, G. Joseph Gorciak, who specialized in Employment & Labor Law. Joe was thoughtful, kind, and listened to my issues as he helped me wade through mounds of paperwork. At one point, I was down to about 82 pounds due to all the worry and stress. Usually, my weight was in the low 90s, so for me to lose ten pounds was too much. Joe's expertise and outgoing supportive presence helped me stick with the long and tedious process.

For months, I had resisted filling out the paperwork, but finally I submitted it in May 2012. After several months of excruciating waiting and worrying, along with lots of handholding by my attorney and supportive family and friends, my disability retirement was approved. My last day at BPA in November 2012 was bittersweet. Without a doubt, I knew I'd miss my friends, but I was happy to be done with full time work and the escalating hardship that came with it.

Goodbye to My Job

My supervisor gave a nice speech on my last day about what a good employee I was. He told a story about how we had to add all the new products into our new billing system and test the contracts to make sure the bills calculated correctly. Everything in the new system needed to be tested and checked. I had been the first one to complete this involved process with all my customers. My boss appreciated and acknowledged all my hard and efficient work, even in my final months at BPA.

Despite this nice ending, I couldn't help but think about why I had rarely been recognized for this at the time I was doing the work. It really would have helped my morale. Annually, BPA holds an awards meeting that lasts half a day, recognizing employees for their hard work. Not once in my last six years at BPA in the billing department did I individually get mentioned. I believe this lack of public acknowledgment and appreciation was part of the reason I lost confidence in myself toward the end of my career. Somehow, I had become invisible in a company where my work ethic and dedication had been in play for 24 years.

When I left the BPA building on my final day, I cried with relief. I was scared because my future was an unknown, but I also felt exhilarated and excited. I thought to myself, *I am taking my first steps toward a new, easier, less stressful life.*

At the same time, it was so odd knowing I would not be back inside that building again, where I had spent most of my adult life.

Chapter 19

A New Life After Retirement

A few weeks after I retired, I moved back to San Diego to be closer to my sisters. After my divorce, I knew there would be a time when I may need help. If so, I'd have family members who could help me. Also, I wanted milder weather that was easier on me physically and mentally. Bottom line, I just wanted a new start at life after my retirement. Joel and I decided he would keep Hoss since he was an old dog, and the journey might be too stressful for him. Hoss lived another two years.

Goodbye Portland, Hello San Diego

With help, I packed all my life's belongings into a U-Haul truck. My Uncle David drove, and I rode shotgun. The whole trip to San Diego, Uncle David called me Miss Daisy, and I called him Hoke. We had lots of laughs on the open road, and it turned into a bonding experience. The downside began when we hit L.A. traffic about 2:30 p.m. on a weekday and didn't get to my dad's house in San Juan Capistrano until about 8:30 p.m. That means it took us about six hours to travel less than 100 miles on Southern California freeways. I had to pee badly and there was no way out of that traffic to find a bathroom. When I asked my uncle if we could stop somewhere, which meant getting off the freeway, he half laughingly snapped, "No fucking way!"

So, we crept along for hours down through Los Angeles and into Orange County, part of an endless river of cars. Finally, I took my uncle's empty coffee cup, pulled my pants down in the cab of the U-Haul, and peed like a rockstar! Didn't even miss the cup—quite an accomplishment for me. After that move, my uncle declared, "You are officially a trucker!

The Responsible One

Public transportation in San Diego is nonexistent compared to Portland, Oregon. In Portland, I didn't need a car, but San Diego is a car culture. I prided myself on being independent, however, I had to admit that I needed more help, especially with transportation. It scared the shit out of me to rely on people; however, this reality has become a part of my life. I decided it took me awhile in Portland and it will take me time here. Not being 100 percent capable of coming and going as I please became fucking scary when I returned to Southern California.

In my family, everyone refers to me as the "the responsible one"—the one with a good head on my shoulders. I think I got that reputation because as a teenager I started worrying I would end up in a nursing home as an old woman, sitting in my pee, waiting for someone to help me. So, early along I made a point to be good with money because I worried I wouldn't have any. Plus, I didn't think I'd find a job or ever have a boyfriend or get married. I figured it was going to be up to me to take care of myself. Ironically, I ended up getting the secure, government job with a pension and medical insurance, and I was married for 16 years!

It seems like my sisters didn't worry about their futures the way I did. When we were young adults, they didn't plan much past tomorrow, and they still don't. In that way, I wish I was more like them. They don't seem

Reunion for Teri, her sisters, and their dad, Brian, 2007.

half as worried as I am about most things. My older sister has worked as a restaurant server since high school, and this has worked fine for her. Tami used to get so pissed off when my parents asked her, "When are you going to get a real job?" as if the job she has is fake. Tami has stayed at her job for years and she's a great server. In addition, she has been in a relationship for more than 30 years with her partner, Matthew, and together, they have created a home and a life.

My twin divorced and became a single mother when her children were young. Traci successfully sold timeshares and later, went on to have a successful career with a law firm where she is now an intake coordinator. To me, it looks like a hard way to live, but she has made it work. Traci has no one to rely on if she needs help—except me. I may not be able to always help her, but I will if I can. In turn, my sisters have said they will be there for me, if I need help.

Too Much Worrying

Returning to San Diego and having my family much closer, intensified so many of my worries and fears. For me, the worst fear is not being able to keep my independence and take care of myself. I see it as a form of failure, and I carry that pressure and I hate

Teri and Traci celebrate their 50th, 2014.

it. Sometimes, I think, *What if I completely fuck up one day? Or decide to run away from everything and throw my cell phone away?*

Honestly, there are days when I'd love that! No pressure, no worries, no more thinking it's my job to hold the family together. All of this, I put on myself, and I just haven't figured out how to let it go—yet.

My family didn't let Nana go into a longterm nursing home, and I'm determined not to go to one either. She had an in-home caregiver during the week. Either my Aunt Carol and Uncle Gary, or Joel and I took care of Nana when the caregivers couldn't. My Aunt Carol's dedication to her mom's care until the end gave me great comfort. I know my family members step up for one another when needed. My worst fear is ending up in a nursing home, but I am also confident my family will help me if they can.

Aunt Carol and Uncle Gary.

Years ago, Tami wrote me a note on a bar napkin in a dark karaoke bar with red walls and carpet. Someone was singing a bad rendition of "Another One Bites the Dust." The note is dated December 8, 1997, and says:

> *This is a promise note that when you are old and grey, you will never be alone. You can always stay with me. I'll take care of you forever, and if you want to lay in a bed in your pee— you can!*
> *Love, Tami*
> *P.S. But I won't let you!*

I still have that note in case I need it for proof. I try to reassure my family that I will be easy to care for. "Just sit me in a chair somewhere; it's not like I'll get up and disappear. I don't eat much either. Just bathe me occasionally, and I'll be good."

Ironically, I believe I worry more about Traci, and if you asked Traci, I think she'd say she worries more about me. Traci worries about my physical well-being, especially as we grow older, and I worry if Traci will be happy and content in her own life. Perhaps this is common among twins—the ongoing worry and intense love for one another in this world that can be a real bitch sometimes.

Teri and her constant companion at Punalu'u Black Sand Beach, Hawaii, 2024.

Chapter 20
My Constant Companions

As much as my family is entwined in most aspects of my life, the equipment I use to move through my life are my daily companions. They offer me essential physical support and freedom.

Years ago, I applied for long-term-care insurance, trying to be proactive if anything were to happen and I couldn't take care of myself. I got turned down for the insurance because I answered "Yes" to one question on the entire application, which was: "Do you use a wheelchair, walker, or scooter?"

I called the insurance company and asked why. They said wheelchairs, walkers, and scooters are not considered durable medical equipment. Naturally, I asked what were they considered? The voice on the other end of the phone said, "Those are considered convenience items."

When I heard that, I angrily snapped back, "I guess I could crawl!" and hung up. Convenience, no! Necessity, yes.

Wheelchair, Scooter, or Walker

I have always had wheelchairs and crutches. Since about the age of 12, I have used a walker. Depending on what I'm doing, where I'm going, and how fast I need to move, I will either use the wheelchair, my scooter, or my walker. For instance, if I'm going to the mall, I'll take my wheelchair. The wheelchair is faster, and I can keep up with people better. If I take my walker everywhere, people will be waiting a long time for me to catch up.

When I use my walker as opposed to my wheelchair or scooter, people treat me differently. One time when I used my walker instead of my scooter on Portland's light rail, familiar people I saw every day when I used my scooter, simply did not recognize me. With the walker, I was standing up and using a different piece of equipment. They looked at me oddly, trying to figure out how they knew me.

When I use my walker, people are less likely to open doors and offer assistance. Depending on what type of equipment I am using, people view me as either more disabled or less disabled. This reinforces my experience that some people still see only the equipment first and not me, as a person.

In 2025, it's depressing that I still have to deal with the public's high level of obliviousness around people with physical challenges and their equipment. I like to think people are more evolved about this than they really are, but I guess it's like common sense not being too common. Ultimately, I decide what equipment to use now, based solely on the ease of what I am doing at the time. I resist letting other people's perceptions influence my decisions.

Repairs

All this equipment requires ongoing repairs and replacements. Getting help when there is a problem has always been an adventure, and medical insurance coverage can be fickle and difficult—or nonexistent. In the early 1990s when I was still driving a car, my friend and I went to a local bar for a drink. When we left, I realized someone had stolen my Quickie black-and-red wheelchair out of the back of my Jeep. Quickie wheelchairs are ultralight, folding, and among the top-of-the-line in the wheelchair biz. At that time, mine had been made specifically for my measurements and cost about $1,000. In the 2020s, these wheelchairs now cost about $3000, or easily more than $7,000 depending on specifications.

My car insurance covered the loss, thankfully, and I got another wheelchair. However, my medical insurance would not get me another one, so it was good that the wheelchair was stolen out of my car. Otherwise, I would've had to buy another one out of pocket.

Scooter Challenges

When I was growing up, scooters were not available; it sure would've made getting around much easier! I got my first electric scooter when I was 23 years old, shortly after I started work at BPA. I used my scooter to travel from my home to Portland's light rail, MAX, and then to BPA headquarters in N.E. Portland where the company provided a scooter for work purposes. The office building is huge and when I started working there, I was on the second floor. The scooter was a substantial help.

I've had numerous problems with different scooters over the years. The first one I had lasted for more than 10 years. I was reluctant to get another one because my first one worked so well. My next scooter was called a Golden Companion. That made me laugh. What a horrible name! I felt like I should be zooming around a nursing home for the elderly on my Golden Companion.

Well, my Golden Companion ended up being a golden lemon! That thing died whenever I was out and about, and most often in the same busy intersection in N.E Portland—crossing 162nd and Burnside—on my daily route to the train stop. For about three years, my Golden Companion nickel-and-dimed me with repair expenses until I finally decided to get a new scooter called Passport Junior. Granted, the name is still ridiculous, but the scooter has continued to serve me for 10 plus years. When I worked at BPA, they provided a scooter, which is the company's practice for those who need them. I specifically told BPA not to buy a Golden Companion. Guess which one they bought? Yup, a Golden Companion! *Why listen to someone who uses them? What could I possibly know?* They are cheaper, but in the long run, BPA spent more money fixing the ultimate lemon of all scooters!

For lunch one day, I met a friend at Nordstrom Café at Lloyd Center, just a couple blocks from my work. For an able-bodied walker, maybe it takes five minutes to get there, but with my scooter it usually took less time if I went full speed, about four miles per hour. It was a rainy November day and a downpour made scooter travel dicey. As I crossed the street in my scooter, there was flooding because of a clogged storm drain. The water was up to about mid-calf area for people walking across the street. I had no choice but to continue crossing the street in my scooter. A man passing by helped push my scooter through the water until I got to the door of Nordstrom Café. Once inside, I made it to the table where my friend was waiting.

After lunch, I tried to leave, but my scooter would not budge. I called the security guards at the BPA building located just a few blocks away to see if they could walk my work scooter over so I could use that to get back to work. For an hour, I sat inside Nordstrom waiting for a security guard to call back. My friend had walked back to BPA to see what was going on. In the meantime, since I hadn't heard anything, I called Joel to see if he could help. Fortunately, he did. It was uncomfortable asking Joel to do this because we were getting a divorce and I didn't want to ask. Still, he drove for more than 20 minutes to pick me up at the café, along with the stalled scooter, and took me back to work. Joel is a good man; he's had my back many times!

Later, I learned that BPA regulations did not allow security guards to help me because "it was against the rules to take my work scooter off government property." This whole debacle with a stalled scooter took more than two hours to resolve. While waiting for someone to help me, I cried from frustration and helplessness.

I understand there are rules and regulations, but in some cases, they are meant to be broken and should be. The problem could have been fixed in maybe 10 minutes. In that situation, the thing that upset me the most was that I had been employed at BPA for almost 24 years and still, they couldn't just step up and help me. After that incident, I kept having this nagging thought about BPA: *They couldn't break that one simple rule for 10 minutes?*

I took my personal scooter to the repair shop and once it had dried out, it ran okay, but not right. When I first turned the scooter on and engaged the throttle, it jerked back, almost popping a wheelie. The repairman told me the whole underside of the scooter was rusted and needed to be replaced. I didn't see what he was looking at because he took my scooter away. The repair shop wanted to charge more than $300. I decided to get a second opinion. The second shop said it wasn't rusted at all, and my scooter was one of the cleanest, well-taken care of scooters they had ever seen. I cancelled everything with the first shop once I got the second opinion.

After my scooter completely dried out, the jerking quit completely and continued to run like a charm for many more years. The smallest things can turn into huge problems. At the same time, some problems could have been avoided with a little communication, teamwork, and human decency. Sometimes, all I can do is cry and wish things were easier. But once I have a good cry, I get over it and I soldier on until the next fiasco. No wonder I swear like a fucking sailor!

Teri and Claus, 2016.

Chapter 21

People with Disabilities Want Sex and Companionship

As an adult, I have dated—and married—great, nice, funny men. Some were good looking, too. Yes, it's true, crippled girls can land hot ones every so often. I write that previous sentence with sarcasm for those who think women like me are unattractive and not sexual. We are!

My friend Headly is in his late 60s, and he has a beard and a long gray ponytail. He wears red Converse sneakers and drinks lots of coffee. For years, Headly took care of his elderly father, Pops, until he died. He is smart, maybe even a genius, and he writes political blogs. We once had a conversation in which he said he was in love with me from the moment we met. I liked him immediately because he's smart, interesting, and tells great stories. Headly told me I was the first girl in a wheelchair whom he thought of, and looked at, in a sexual way. "You are the kind of dirty-mouthed, funky, hippie chick I've always wanted," he admitted. "Then I got to know you and I realized it was about more than just the packaging."

That kind of observation is another reason why I decided to write this book. I wonder how common it is that most people don't look at handicapped people as sexual. Unfortunately, I think it's extremely common. This is sad. There are probably millions of sexual beings out there trapped in bodies that don't work exactly right, and people assume just aren't sexual.

Being Sexual Is Being Human

Expression of one's sexuality is a huge part of having a complete life that many people with disabilities miss out on. I believe that everyone who wants it, should have fun, sexy experiences in their lives. It's what makes life exciting. For me, it's important my partner desires me as a sexual being. It's all part of wanting to feel human, to feel normal—whatever that is!

After my divorce, my big insecurity about being in another relationship was, *Will I be enough sexually for a man?* It's not like I can swing from chandeliers to have sex or perform different Kama Sutra positions. My sexual positions are limited. Physically, I can't do some things that I want to do, so I try to make it up in other ways—but I still worry.

I don't want my sex life to get boring; I believe boring sex kills a relationship. Yet, as I get older, I realize there is more to a relationship than sex. When I am an old woman, my man better like me as a person because a pretty face and body don't last.

Love Is Essential

In addition to worries about being sexually satisfying, I also have big trust issues. To this day, I have a hard time believing a man when he says, "I love you." When I hear that, I think, *Maybe he's just saying that because he's being nice or he doesn't want to hurt my feelings.* Or I worry, *He might get tired of me.*

I know what I want in a relationship, and I know what will make me happy. Most importantly, I want to have someone who truly loves and accepts me—all my good qualities, along with my challenging aspects. And regardless of his moods, I can tell he loves me and means it. It's also important that my partner wants to include me on his adventures. I don't want to be automatically sidelined because I have physical challenges.

More than once, I've been told being in a relationship with me was too much because I have cerebral palsy. "Too much" can mean emotionally, yet also physically. Men I have had relationships with have had to physically pick me up a lot and help me get upstairs, or into a big truck, or get to some place that is not accessible to people with wheelchairs or walkers.

In situations with physical barriers, I feel bad instantly, but there's nothing I can do. So, do I worry the relationship will end because of that, too? Yes. I must admit it's always in the back of my mind. Someday, I hope I can stop worrying about these things and become more secure in a romantic relationship.

Claus

Once I was settled in San Diego, I enjoyed going to a local bar where Tami and her boyfriend, Matthew, have worked for more than 20 years. One night at the bar someone very interesting unexpectedly popped into my life. Tami kept making me stand up and show people the cute dress I was wearing. Fun banter kept the group lively, and one man in the group said in a deep voice with an accent, "You look like a million-bucks and talk like 50 cents."

Immediately, I thought, *That's so funny!*

I didn't think of it as a negative statement. If you know me, that is a true statement—although not always the million-bucks part! Instantly, we clicked. Claus is a tall man, 6' 2", from Bavaria, Germany. Talking with him that first evening, I soon learned he has a motorcycle and considers himself to be a biker. I could also tell he had a big, soft heart. Claus's humor made me easily laugh and he was interesting. I loved hearing stories about his life and in turn, he was interested in my stories. From the start, our conversation was easy and engaging.

We talked about Germany and the nightlife on Reeperbahn, considered Hamburg's most famous street. Restaurants, nightclubs, bars, sex shops, and brothels are some of the major businesses on Reeperbahn. Claus was surprised I knew about this famous street and later, he told me that's what hooked him. "What are the odds I'd be sitting in a bar in Chula Vista, California and meet a girl like you, who knows about Reeperbahn? It was crazy! The planets must have been aligned!"

Claus also told me that when he first saw me, he didn't notice anything physically different. As he explained it, "When I first saw you, I just thought you were a beautiful girl with dark dreadlocks and a smile that could stop a bus full of nuns!"

His description made me laugh and it drew me to him. This was the beginning of something big!

Another Serious Relationship

It was great to have someone in my life once again to laugh with, and dream with, and make plans for a future together. It was also great to have an active sex life again. At first, we got to know each other on Matthew and Tami's brown leather couch. The first time we had sex, the way Claus touched me blew my mind. It was so gentle, and I got goosebumps all over. Later, he told me, "Someday, I want to buy that couch for nostalgia's sake."

Not long after we met, Claus went to dinner with an ex-girlfriend. She asked if he was seeing anyone. Claus told her about me, and he told her that I was disabled. According to Claus, the ex-girlfriend laughed hard and said she didn't believe it—at first. She couldn't imagine Claus dating someone with a physical disability.

When Claus shared this story with me, I wasn't surprised when he described the ex-girlfriend laughing. Women have that reaction a lot. He then showed the former girlfriend photos of me. Her response was, "She must be amazing, or you wouldn't let her in your life."

Probably what I like best about Claus is that he treats me like a regular person in all ways. He'll say things like, "Pinky, a beer would be nice." As odd as this may sound, it feels good when Claus asks me to get him a beer. No boyfriend has ever asked me to get up and get him something.

Every so often my old insecurities come up and some days when Claus is being honest with me about something and just speaking his truth, I get worried and think, *It seems we won't be together that long.* Then on other days, when my confidence is up, I feel like it will be forever.

Living on a Boat

My living situation during the first two years in San Diego was on a boat with Claus. There were some nice things about it. For starters, I didn't need a walker when I moved about the 45-foot ketch. The interior is solid teak wood and there are lots of things to hold onto. I get around inside effortlessly. It's kind of like camping; everything is nearby. I can easily reach dishes and cabinets. Anyone who knows me would not believe the size of my closet when I lived on the boat. It was small, no room for extra clothes. I decided I liked the minimalist approach; less to keep track of.

The boat is cozy, but there are some challenges. I can't easily get on and off and leave as I please. Getting from the boat onto the dock by myself is problematic. I pull myself up using the bar on the bimini, a canvas sunshade, to the edge of the boat where Claus lifts me up

Teri seeing the sites in Ensenada, Mexico, 2014.

and puts me on the dock. Also, when I first moved on the boat, I couldn't get from the cabin out to the topside. There is a small, five-rung ladder for climbing in and out of the cabin. The steps are spaced just far enough apart that I can't lift my leg that high. With practice, I could pull myself up the ladder to the outside, using just my arms! I have amazing upper body strength, but now that I'm older, I can't do it anymore alone. Now, when we're on the boat, Claus assists me. We talked about getting a lift installed, but that wasn't possible. We eventually moved, but Claus still owns the boat and we still sail.

In 2014, we moved to a house Claus has owned for years. It's in the mountains east of the city. I like the house, but it is in a rural area, and this presents transport problems for me, causing friction in our relationship at times. Again, it comes back to accessibility and transportation. My independent streak wants to get into San Diego when I want, not when someone can drive me.

"I'm Not Being Nosey, But..."

Claus told me that since we've been together, he notices how different people react when they see us together versus when he was with a former girlfriend who didn't have a physical disability. I'm sure it is something to get used to.

We laugh about people's reactions sometimes. A good example is the neighbors, Tony and Tim, whom we met when we lived on the boat. Tony is an older man with a long grey ponytail and a beer belly. One day he saw us walking by his boat and struck up a conversation. Ever since then, when Tony sees Claus, he asks about me. The second time Tony saw Claus at the boat dock, he asked, "Where's Teri?" Followed with, "If you don't mind me asking, how'd you end up with her? How did you meet"?

Claus said, "I actually met her in a bar."

The next time Tony asked Claus, "Not that I'm being nosey, but what happened to her?"

Claus responded, "I don't know, I think she has CP." When we first met, Claus didn't ask me about CP. As he likes to say, "I just thought you were slow on the hoof!" It was refreshing that when we met, Claus didn't immediately ask, "What's wrong with you?"

When people start a sentence with "Hope you don't mind…" or "I'm not being nosey, but …" that's usually exactly what they are being. I try to cut people slack and chalk it up to curiosity, but it does get old.

Recently, Claus was talking to Tony and once again, he asked where I was. Standing next to Tony on the dock was Tim, an older grey-haired, redneck type. When Tony mentioned me, Tim chimed in, "Oh, your sister, right?"

Claus said he just gave Tim a look, not even honoring the stupid question with an answer. He told me Tim's response showed him that guys like Tim would be completely incapable of having a relationship with someone like me. It's just completely out of their realm of thinking. The odd thing about all of this is that Claus and I had been on Tim's boat not long before this conversation, having a drink with Tim, his wife, and some of their friends. I thought it was pretty evident

Teri and her best friend Kelly.

that Claus and I were an affectionate couple. The other people on the boat were certainly aware of this.

It's not uncommon for people to assume I'm the sister, not the girlfriend, of my significant other. My whole life I've said sarcastically, "Crippled people don't have any friends, only their brothers and sisters are friendly with them."

Even my best friend, Kelly, used to say all the time it was unbelievable how people thought we were sisters. How could I possibly just have a friend who wanted to hang out with me? She had to be my sister!

Claus is afraid that someday he's going to have to punch someone because he gets so sick and tired of seeing people stare and act strangely when they see us together. More than once, I've walked into a bar, sat on a barstool, and watched people next to me move away. Claus can tell that some people have no problem, and then there are others who get weird. "More than anything, I think people are curious," Claus explained. "Meeting you has really opened my eyes to other people."

Claus told me when he is in Germany, he sees people in wheelchairs everywhere. It's not uncommon to see people with disabilities working in many different situations. It surprises him, or at least he notices right away, how people react to me in public in the United States. Plus, he's surprised at the things people say to me. That's why Claus has constantly reminded me of why I needed to write this book.

Feel Like an Alien

A few months after Claus and I got together, we took a road trip to Arizona on Claus's motorcycle. One morning, we met some of his friends for breakfast. We walked in together to join the group already at the table. As I walked to the table, the server saw me and announced to the waiting breakfast party, "Here comes the girl with the walker."

When I turned the corner, everyone was staring. I felt like I should pause before sitting down, wave like a beauty queen on a parade float, and say, "Hello, it's me, the girl with the walker. Please continue with your meal."

Sometimes, I feel like an alien. If anyone else had been in front of me, how would the server have described them? I think she'd just say, "Here comes the rest of your party." It's as if the normal people of the world refuse to let people with physical disabilities be anything beyond their handicap. Just when I start to feel like myself, I get someone like that server saying something about my physical disability and I'm reminded, "Oh shit! That's right, I forgot. I can't walk."

Then I feel self-conscious all over again. I don't think every minute of every day, "I can't walk." I just go about my day. It's usually someone else saying something about my disability or the way I move or my equipment that reminds me, *Oh fuck, that's right.*

Claus hopes that all the questions won't get to him one day. Uhhhh...me, too, babe! I'd hate to lose him because he just gets burnout from people continuously making ignorant comments about me or our relationship.

Getting away from it all, salmon fishing in Alaska, 2022.

Chapter 22
Navigating Prejudice and Obliviousness

After a lifetime of enduring insensitive comments, bizarre questions, and offensive actions as a person with a disability, I knew I had to write a book. It had all piled up on top of my feelings. My book has been my therapy, and my hope to enlighten the "norms"—able-bodied people—of what it is like to move through this world with mobility issues. I'd extend this to anyone who has faced emotional or intellectual disabilities, as well. And a reminder to readers that one accident, illness, or traumatic experience and you could end up joining this group of millions.

Condescending Compliments

Comments meant to be kind and nice mostly come across as backhanded compliments. In our society, when you have a physical handicap, the success bar is usually quite low. If disabled people can get out of bed and get dressed every day, able-bodied people comment on how "inspirational" and "amazing" they are.

When people see me, they want to tell me what an "inspiration" I am for them in their own lives. This is not a compliment to me. I am not living to inspire able-bodied people; I am just living my life as best as I can. Regularly, people say, "You have a great attitude Teri, you get along great, and you have amazing determination and perseverance."

And, of course, they'll add, "And you have such a charming personality!" Trust me, these are not compliments!

Infantilizing People with Disabilities

Some people can be patronizing when they talk to me, especially if I'm sitting in a wheelchair or on a scooter. Throughout my adult life, I have had people treat me as if I'm a child, referring to me as "kiddo" and "sweetie" and patting me on the head like a dog. This can get extra irritating because the people doing this are usually a lot younger than me.

I know people think they are just being nice, but I experience it as condescending. It gets annoying at a certain age—adulthood! I don't see able-bodied adults patting each other on the head. Maybe it's because I'm sitting most of the time, plus I'm petite, and some people think of me as a kid. Even in my early 60s, I'm still amazed with how some people speak to me as if I'm a child. Or worse, they talk to the person I am with instead of talking directly to me. One evening when Joel and I were having dinner at a restaurant, the server took Joel's order and then asked him, "What does she want?"

Joel said, "I don't know, ask her."

This happens more often than you might think. Another time, Claus and I were at a pharmacy picking up my prescription, waiting to talk with the pharmacist. When the pharmacist looked at us, he immediately started asking Claus questions about my medical needs, even though I was right there, my insurance card in hand. It was as if I was invisible, or a small child who could not speak for myself. These situations arise regularly, and I automatically speak up. Honestly, I believe many people aren't even aware they do this. The prejudices and stereotypes about disabled people are deeply ingrained in our culture.

Another situation in which I feel like the invisible woman is when I am out with friends and we meet a stranger who just starts talking with them about me as if I am not even there. Recently at the grocery store, this guy asked Claus, "What happened to her?"

I was standing right in front of him, stunned in disbelief! Claus blurted out, "Oh, she was a pilot in a plane crash!"

I almost burst out laughing. The guy looked amazed and said, "Wow!" Then asked, "Civilian or military?"

We like to fuck with people who ask stupid questions.

There are times when I do not think people listen to me, especially if I am sitting in my wheelchair or on my scooter. For example, I was waiting outside a friend's work one day when a car drove up and a passenger asked a bystander where a particular place was located. When I heard their question, I yelled loudly enough for them to hear me say, "It's right here," as I pointed at the door. They looked at me, drove past, and found another person to ask. Again, it was a prime example of people assuming I don't know anything because I have a physical disability. Now, there's also the possibility that because I am a woman they assumed I knew nothing about directions. In truth, I am bad at directions, but in this case, I was standing right outside the place they were looking for!

I have to maintain a good sense of humor and an ability to laugh at certain things as well as laugh at myself. Otherwise, I will be a recluse, crying in my beer daily. Sometimes, it's okay if I make fun of myself; believe me, I have lots of material. But there are times when I just don't want to laugh, or talk, or even respond to stupid statements. Sometimes, I just want to yell out, "You're hurting me, stop!"

Invading My Space

People feel they can approach me and say, or ask, almost anything they want. Perhaps they see my physical vulnerability and think it's open season for saying whatever they want. Some people seem to latch on to something about me and it just progresses from there. If I'm in the mood, I go along with the questioning and see it as an interesting social experiment.

Sometimes it's funny, sometimes it's annoying, and sometimes it just pisses me off. Other times, I'm just tired of it all and I already know what's coming before the questions even start. Must be my intuition. Usually, I just try to reassure people I am fine, and I have a good life.

Many scars grace my body due to several operations as a child. I even have some scars on my head from falling. For some reason, complete strangers think it's okay to say or ask me anything about my body, no matter how personal.

Regularly, I rode light rail in Portland for my job at BPA. One hot summer day I boarded MAX wearing a short sundress with sandals. Rarely do I wear short dresses without boots because my leg muscles are atrophied and I consider them unattractive. I want to say ugly, but I'm trying to be kind in my self-descriptions. Still, I am self-conscious about my bare legs. Sitting quietly, I noticed all the other commuters were minding their own business. Suddenly, this White guy said to me with a hillbilly twang at the top of his lungs, "Hey, did you know you have a scar on your leg? What's that from?"

I just pretended I didn't hear him, as I often do when I don't want to deal with people. He kept at it. Finally, I looked down at my legs and in my best sarcastic voice said, "Gee, I never noticed. Look at that!"

He shut right up. Other passengers just looked at the whole scene in disbelief. A couple people smiled after my comment, as if they were about to laugh.

Most of the time, strangers seem to think it's okay to invade my space. Perhaps my diminutive stature, combined with my equipment, make me seem like an easy target. One day a man felt compelled to sing a Motown love song in my ear while we were on MAX. Annoyed, I tried to disengage from him, but he kept insisting that I liked it and kept asking me if I liked it. A passenger intervened on my behalf; he had to tell this man to leave me alone.

Another time, a young man dressed in sweats and a T-shirt that looked like they hadn't been washed for quite some time, got on the train and sat down across the aisle from me. He was wearing a baseball cap, hiding his greasy, dark hair that peeked out from under his cap. He said, "Hey, I never see beautiful girls in scooters."

Ignoring him, I kept playing a game on my phone. It was embarrassing, and the train was quiet. Then he added, "Oh, I bet no one's ever flirted with you before."

I couldn't believe it when he said that, but I didn't answer. I thought to myself, *Amazing, you have no fucking idea, and you know nothing about my life.*

A part of me wanted to say, "I bet more people have flirted with me than they have with your stinking ass." Then I would've stuck my tongue out, as if to say, "So there!" But I just wanted him to leave me alone, so I said nothing.

Sometimes, strangers get emotional when they see me with my scooter or wheelchair or using my walker. The drunk ones really feel it! In 2002, I got my sisters, cousins, and their significant others to all meet in Las Vegas. There was an Aerosmith concert in town and besides, I wanted to get my family together after some long absences. Not everyone went with me to the concert, but everyone showed up in Vegas.

One night, Tami, Traci, my niece Alix, my husband at the time, Joel, and I went for a walk around old Vegas. I was in my wheelchair, rolling along, enjoying the warm night air and being with family. Suddenly, this drunk man approached us and started asking what was wrong with me. He wanted to tell me that he made custom wheelchairs. We politely engaged him for about five minutes and finally, he left—or so we thought. A few minutes later, he returned with a glass rose and handed it to me, sobbing, telling me through his tears, "Poor Teri. Please let me help you."

Then he turned to my sisters and pleaded, "Please take care of Teri." I reassured him, "I'm fine. Don't worry!"

The drunk stranger went on and on about me, and his life's work. We kept trying to leave, but he kept after us. My niece, Alix, who was 14 at the time, was stunned by this whole scene. She kept asking, "Why is he doing this?" Then after a bit, she said, "I feel sorry for him. He loves you Aunt Teri!"

I told Alix this happens all the time with me. This was the first time Alix had witnessed it, so she was a bit stunned that the public would approach me that way and say the things they do. We were all kind of nervously laughing while this was carrying on, and after about another 10 minutes, the drunk man finally collected himself and went on his way!

Shortly after that, another drunk man started walking toward us. This time, Tami just said, "Ok, we are leaving—here comes another one!" She pushed my wheelchair faster and we escaped the next scene.

The good news is that Las Vegas weekend was a success for our family get together. By the end of it, we were crying and hugging one other, saying, "I love you!"

I noted, "Aerosmith always brings people together!"

Do You Really Have a Job?

Countless people seemed to be surprised that I had a job, and they had no reservations about telling me so. "Where are you going?" one commuter asked me at 6 a.m. on the way to work.

I said, "To work."

"Oh, you have a job? I figured you were going shopping."

I wondered, *Who goes shopping at 6 in the fucking morning?*

"Where do you work?"

"I work at BPA."

Most of the time, the response would be one of amazement, "Oh, really!" It often felt like people couldn't believe that I had a real job and contributed to society. Then they would say, "Well, that's nice, or fun for you."

My usual response to that statement would be, "It's a job. I hate mine as much as anyone else." In truth, I didn't hate my job, but I said that because usually people complain about their jobs. My hope was to make them see I'm like anyone else. I'd rather still be sleeping.

Often, I thought, *These people would really freak out if they knew I probably make more money than they do!*

The cynic in me believes they expected me to tell them I worked at Goodwill sorting paper clips or something. That way, they could feel more comfortable with the idea that I worked at a paid job!

Speaking of Goodwill, to this day I cringe every time I see Goodwill commercials that focus on handicapped employees. It's like they're doing them a big favor because no one else will hire them. Plus, this kind of advertising reinforces the belief that a simple job is the only job we "special needs" people are qualified to handle. It dismisses the truth that all kinds of competent people work at resale stores, including Goodwill.

Bullying

When I was young, there was always the kid that walked by me, contorted his face, and slapped his hand against his chest, making the "retard" sound and then call me retarded. That's happened more times in my life than I can count. As a kid, I always shouted back, "I'm not retarded!"

This retard gesture is the same one the 45th president of the United States used when mocking the *New York Times'* reporter who has a congenital disability. To this day, I don't understand how that presidential candidate got away with making fun of someone with a physical disability—and then got elected president, twice!

As an adult, the bullying continues. When I worked at BPA, Portland's big shopping center was Lloyd Center. During my lunch break, I'd usually eat at the mall and wander around. One day, I was headed down the sidewalk on my scooter when two twenty-something guys walked toward me. They parted so I could pass between them. As we passed one another, each of them got within an inch of my face and let out a deep, screaming noise. It happened fast, startled me, and I jumped. They laughed loudly and kept walking. I think I yelled, "Fuckers!"

The whole incident shocked my system and for the rest of the day I was upset. Usually, I'm not easily bothered, but that scared me, and once I was alone, I cried.

After that incident, I decided adults can be just as bad as the kids who bullied me growing up. My hope was that this kind of bullying and harassment would've stopped when I was an adult. Wrong!

Many times, I tried to board the MAX train like everyone else at rush hour. The doors would open, revealing a car packed with commuters, and someone would shout, "Oh, you can't get on the train, it's too full."

Countless times I had to shout back, "I have to get home just like you!"

MAX has clearly designated spots for people with physical disabilities and space for their wheelchairs, or whatever their mode of transport. Giant images of wheelchairs displayed on the floor and wall designate these spots. Signs are also on the windows, stating that commuters need to please give up their seat for seniors or people with disabilities. And at every stop, there is a similar announcement over the loudspeaker drawing commuters' attention to the special seating.

Do you think people pay attention? Some do, but not as many as one might think. Even funnier—or sadder, depending on your perspective—is the passenger who sits and ignores every fucking clue to give up his or her seat. When I would approach, the able-bodied commuter would look up and say, "Oh, do you want me to move?"

And once he moved, he bitched about the inconvenience under his breath. To be honest, after more than 20 years of riding public transportation, I was tired of asking people to move out of spots designated as handicapped seating, not only to make room for people like me, but to not block the aisles or doors.

Religious Fanatics

Another segment of the population that seems drawn to me are religious people who tell me, "God only picks special people to be like you."

Or they ask, "Are you saved? You won't have any pain in heaven." Or the most embarrassing situation is when they stand there in public and pray "with" me.

My favorite story about religious fanatics is the one who approached me when I was walking into a Hallmark store. This lady held the door open as I maneuvered my walker. I said, "Thank you." As she held the door, she started telling me, "You should come to my church because they heal people."

For a moment I paused in the doorway, looked at her, and said, "Don't you think if that was really true you would have a line, miles long, around your church and this would somehow be big news?"

She didn't like my response and promptly let go of the heavy glass door, almost knocking me off my feet. Stunned by her rudeness, I turned and said, "That's not very Christian-like."

I only said that because I have heard that same thing countless times from other religious types. I can't believe people buy into that stuff. I mean, I have heard of faith and it's a good thing—maybe it could cure a headache, but something tells me CP is a bit tougher. I don't know, call me crazy.

One night, I was waiting for the train home after a movie. A guy in his twenties approached me and began talking. This was the gist of our conversation:

"Hi, can I pray with you?"

"That's not really my thing, but thanks."

"Why not?"

"I'm agnostic."

"What's agnostic?"

"Basically, that means I'll believe it when I see it."

He persisted. "What if you saw a miracle like someone was healed? Would you believe?"

Sighing, I told him, "I get that a lot. It would have to be pretty fucking amazing to get me to be a believer."

Then he said, "I didn't mean anything because you are...." He paused, pointing at my scooter. "I just saw you from over in the park, and me and my friends wanted to pray with you."

"Believing in God to me is like Santa and the Easter Bunny," I responded. "But that's just me. You can believe what you want, I will too."

Then he smiled and started to walk away, saying, "You're awesome!"

Another time, I was sitting on the motorcycle outside a small store, waiting for Claus who was buying snacks. A young blond guy in skinny jeans approached and asked, "Can I pray for you?"

"I don't need it," I said, but I let him pray because I thought it was going to be funny. He started praying and rubbing the top of my thigh. I said, "You don't need to rub my thigh to pray."

He continued the prayer. When finished, he asked "Do you feel any different?"

"Not yet, I'll let you know."

You Aren't Going to Believe *This* One!

When I was working 12-hour, rotating shifts at BPA, selling electrical power on real time, my hours were either 6:00 am to 6:00 pm, or the reverse. Utilities from around the Northwest would call hourly, needing to buy power to support their loads. Sometimes, we called utilities looking to buy power, based on the time of year, or what was happening on the system. Usually, I had three days off in a row. One weekday morning when I was off, I decided to visit a friend, so I called a cab. When the cab driver arrived, I started out the front door with my walker. The cabby immediately said, "Come on clippity clop, let's go."

Unsure how to respond to that rude comment, I said nothing and got in the cab. The driver made small talk for a few minutes, then asked, "Are you a stripper?"

I could not believe he asked that. "You have weird work hours, so I figured you must be a stripper."

I wanted to say, "It takes me about 20 minutes to get my clothes off, so people would probably fall asleep while I was stripping."

Instead, I decided not to say anything because he creeped me out. I just wanted to get out of the cab.

Later that night, I told my husband, Joel, about the exchanges with the cabby. He got really pissed off and called the cab company to report the incident. They didn't say much other than apologize.

Inappropriate, disrespectful, thoughtless statements can come my way on any day, anytime, anywhere.

Chapter 23
Civil Rights for the Disabled

People with disabilities face prejudices that are based on a history of exclusion. It wasn't that long ago that our society recommended institutionalizing people like me; born with a physical deformity and considered useless. I was a baby to institutionalize and then submit to forced sterilization as an adult. These decisions were based on misinformation or no information, stereotypes, false assumptions—whatever people in charge determined should be done with people like me. They pre-determined I wouldn't amount to much and advised my family to give me up.

It was the Nanas of the world, and parents, and intelligent, independently functioning adults with disabilities who demanded more. Families, advocates, lawyers, and politicians forged what is called the "de-institutionalization wave" of the 1970s and 1980s. This awakening to the societal discrimination of people with disabilities eventually led to Congress passing crucial civil rights legislation for disabled people in the United States.

Americans with Disabilities Act

For those of you who don't know, the acronym ADA stands for the Americans with Disabilities Act. In 1990, Congress enacted this civil rights legislation to ensure that people with disabilities have the same rights and opportunities as everyone else. This legislation covers jobs, schools, transportation, and many other areas of public life, including accessible public bathrooms. The law was also meant to encourage the employment of people with disabilities.

It's been my experience that, although some places do a good job of making things accessible, the majority of public places are a joke, doing only the bare minimum required by law. I continuously face barriers in public places. In this chapter, I included a few statistics, but mostly I describe my own experiences as one of millions who are disabled and continuously facing barriers.

The Center for Disease Control (CDC), Disability and Health Branch, estimates that more than one in four people living in the United States has some kind of disability. That translates into about 26 percent of the population or about 67 million people. For my group, mobility challenges—people who have serious difficulty walking or climbing stairs—a little more than 12 percent of the population is affected. So, imagine if you will, every day there are millions of us looking for an accessible bathroom when we are out and about. This is our world. And if you are a woman, a person of color, a member of the LGBTQ+ community, you face even more discrimination due to systemic inequities in healthcare and socio-economic barriers, just to name a few! And if you live in a rural area, disability rates are even higher, often linked to lack of medical care and transportation.

Trying to Pee in an Inaccessible World

One of life's most basic needs is to have a place to pee. I can't tell you how many times I've gone to a restaurant, assured there is an accessible bathroom, and still face barriers. Just because the little wheelchair picture on the bathroom door indicates all is well, not necessarily so! Oftentimes, the door to the bathroom weighs more than me, and they are difficult to open. Once I'm in the bathroom, most of the time I am unable to close the stall door because my wheelchair or walker does not fit.

Honestly, when I am in public and need to pee, it's easier to find a hidden spot outside; open the car door, pull my pants down, and pee. When you gotta go, you gotta go. It's the worst feeling to have to pee and not be able to get yourself to a bathroom independently.

Not until able-bodied people become disabled, which could happen on any given day, will they understand the frustration of trying to find a bathroom they can get into. Many times, I've peed my pants in public because I could not find an accessible bathroom. When I go out with friends, I can't relax and have fun until I know the bathroom situation. If it's an easy bathroom that I can get into, I am a happy camper and can proceed with enjoying my evening. If that bathroom is not easily accessible, my evening is basically over.

My favorite bathrooms are the ones with just one toilet and an automatic button to open the door. Let's face it, most Americans are lazy and would appreciate automatic buttons and big bathrooms anyway. I know this because able-bodied people are using the handicapped stall!

Stairs as a Barrier

In 2004 when I went to Washington, D.C. and New York City for my fortieth birthday, we went shopping in Georgetown. I was especially interested in the Diesel apparel store. Unfortunately, there were steps to get to the second floor and the shoe department. I had to wait on the main floor and watch the salesclerk run up and down the stairs, bringing me shoes to try on. That day, I did buy a cute pair of shoes because I liked them, not just because the salesclerk had to go up and down the stairs numerous times. In the past, I have bought unwanted items out of a sense of obligation and guilt because an employee had climbed the stairs way too many times.

After shopping, we stopped at an old bar in the heart of Georgetown to eat and have a beer. Naturally, I had to pee. Guess where the bathroom was? Up a steep flight of stairs. Joel ended up carrying me up the stairs to the bathroom. Once he got me up the stairs, I told him I'd just open the bathroom door and walk inside holding on to the counter and walls. Well, just my fucking luck—I opened the heavy bathroom door, walked in, and now faced more steps leading up to the stalls! That was a first. At that point, I had to pee so badly I just told myself, *Fuck me!* I opened the door and asked Joel to help me again! Can I possibly explain how frustrating it is to be in a situation where I can't go to the bathroom by myself?

I realize that the ADA grandfathered in old buildings as far as making them accessible but at least make it possible to pee! At the time, I thought, *This is ironic. Basically, I am in the nation's capital where Congress passed the ADA and it is one of the least accessible places!*

The Georgetown bar is in the heart of a college town, so it did cross my mind that lots of drunk college students probably make that trek upstairs to the bathroom, nightly. I bet they'd like easier access, too!

Bus Fiasco

On that same trip, we rode a D.C. city bus. Our stop was at the airport where we planned to catch a shuttle to our hotel room. I had my wheelchair and clicked it into the clamp used to secure chairs on the bus. When we got to the airport stop, I tried to unlatch my wheel and get off the bus. The latch was stuck closed. We could not free the chair. The bus driver kept asking if we were getting off. I said, "Not if I can't get the chair released."

Trying to free the latch went on for over an hour. There was a line of people waiting to board the bus and they grew increasingly impatient, as was I. A man sitting behind me was aware of my frustration, probably hearing me use many variations of the word fuck! Suddenly, he pulled long pliers from his jeans' pocket. I burst out laughing, and so did he. He also joined in on my swearing, finally declaring, "Fuck it, pry it open with these motherfuckers."

"Who carries pliers in their pocket?" I asked, still laughing.

Just as Joel was about to use the pliers on the latch, the driver said, "No, don't damage the bus. I will get fired."

By now, the bus driver was on the phone with a supervisor and the two of them were trying to figure out what to do. When the bus driver hung up the phone, she suggested we release the tire of my wheelchair from the frame, and it would be mailed to me later.

"Really? Mailed?" I said, astonished by her suggestion. "Great idea, but how am I supposed to use a wheelchair without the fucking wheel?"

While we were going back and forth with the driver, Joel had been messing with the latch the whole time. Then the driver told us, "No one ever uses those latches because they don't work."

Finally, over an hour later, Joel got the rusted button on the latch to release. Everyone on the bus and in line to get on the bus, clapped and cheered as we left, free at last!

Steps in the Movie Theatre

Remember the old movie theaters where the ramp was the center aisle? The new movie theaters now have steps going down both sides of the theater. The row in the center of the theater is where disabled people can sit. One problem, most often these seats are taken up by able-bodied people who stretch their legs out with a big trough of popcorn on their bellies. More times than not, I have had to use my walker to get down the steps to find a seat elsewhere. Able-bodied people sitting in seats designated for the handicapped had no problem watching me hunt for a seat. Rarely does anyone bother to say, "Would you like to sit here?"

The wheelchair picture on the seat where they were sitting meant nothing to them. When an able-bodied person sits in a theatre seat designated for someone with a handicap, I think an alarm should go off with a recorded voice saying, "Hey, dumb shit, please move your ass to a different seat. Thank you for your cooperation."

Hiring the Disabled

In addition to improving accessibility for people with disabilities, the ADA legislation is intended to encourage businesses to hire people with disabilities, and support people looking for meaningful employment. Unfortunately, the law hasn't closed the huge gap in hiring disabled people. Based on current statistics, and based on what I personally experience, regularly, there is still a huge gap. When I would tell an able-bodied stranger I had a job, I got reactions of disbelief.

In my opinion, to this day it's far from the norm for people with physical handicaps to get mainstream office jobs that pay well. Walk into any business and look around. If you see an employee with a disability, you'll be surprised. The day people have no reaction to seeing someone with a handicap working in mainstream jobs, that is when it will be the norm.

The National Institute on Disability, Independent Living, and Rehabilitation Research (NIDILRR) publishes an annual report on people with disabilities in America. The report in 2024, which captured statistics for 2022, shows significant ongoing gaps between those with disabilities and those without disabilities. The report looks at numerous categories, including employment, earnings from work, health insurance, poverty, and more. The disparities are more like Grand Canyons—far too wide for bridges. When I look at these disparities, I think disabled people are far less valued and suffer economically far more than people without disabilities in the United States. Personally, I see this reflected in numerous different anecdotal ways in my daily life.

Despite passage of significant civil rights legislation in 1990, and strengthened in 2008, things are not looking good for disabled people. According to the report, the gap in the "employment-to-population ratio for civilians ages 18 to 64 living in the community" shows about 34 percent lower employment rate for people with disabilities. As for earnings from work, all things being equal, the report shows a whopping disparity in earnings of about $8,331 for a disabled worker vs. a nondisabled worker. This translates to more than 14 percent more disabled people living in poverty than nondisabled people. With these kinds of real numbers, it is discouraging for those of us with disabilities. Our civil rights as full members of our community and society are not being addressed, respected, and enforced.

Until hiring disabled people becomes the norm, I believe people like me will only get good paying jobs when they are lucky enough to run into people who are smart enough to give them a chance. A variety of companies need to step up and give disabled people real opportunities, and not just lip service on the applications! Saying they do not discriminate against race, sex, age or disability is still wishful thinking!

Teri in Freiburg, Germany, 2025.

Chapter 24
International Travel

Throughout my adult life I've made a point to travel a lot, often internationally. If I had listened to other people telling my what I can and can't do, I probably would've been a recluse most of the time. But my inner determination has always led me to be a part of the world and do things I wanted.

My travels have taken me to Europe, Asia, North America, and the South Pacific, using all forms of transportation, including planes, trains, light rail, cars, buses, taxis, motorcycles, ferries, paddleboats, sailboats, and ships. As I finish this book, I am preparing for a trip from New York City across the Atlantic to England on an ocean liner.

A Love for Travel

People's responses amuse me when I tell them I knew I wanted to take risks, travel, and live my life fully— just like anyone else! I was raised to think independently, and my family treated me like I was physically normal, so why wouldn't I want to travel and have adventures? I don't want to die wishing I had done these things.

Early along, I asked myself, *Why shouldn't I try that? Why not travel?*

New places, interesting people, different cultures, breathtaking environments—all of these fascinate me.

I want to drink in life and savor it. I'm saving the stay-at-home activities like scrapbooking and crafts for when I'm old.

In 1992, I went on my first international vacation that required a passport. My mom and I decided to take a trip to Tahiti. We stayed in a *Fantasy Island*-type resort with sandy paths leading up to our thatched-roof bungalow. The exotic tropical setting looked exactly like an episode of *Lifestyles of the Rich and Famous.* Earlier that year, I had broken up with my first boyfriend, Max, and I was working full time at BPA. A vacation was sorely needed.

The most depressing part about our Tahitian getaway was that it was such a romantic place—and there I was with my mom! We spent our evenings at the Molokai Bar sipping a rum drink called Blue Pacific. One night, I was so buzzed I decided to head back to the bungalow along the sandy path. A screw fell out of my walker while I was walking. This particular screw kept my walker from collapsing. Standing on the pathway, clearly a damsel in distress, a handsome local whom I had met a few times, asked if I needed help. He was wearing only swimming trunks and showing off his tribal tattoos. He ended up carrying me to the bungalow. Later, that same guy carried me back to my bungalow after a day on the water in a paddleboat. As we passed by people who looked at us a bit oddly, he would say, "She is Miss Moorea."

Moorea is a stunningly beautiful volcanic island in French Polynesia, northwest of Tahiti. Later, I learned mo'orea means yellow lizard in Tahitian, based on a legend of how the island came into existence. I also learned the island's original name was Eimeo, the island of beauty. That made me happy.

On the last day as the ferry left the island, I cried because I knew I might not return to this tropical paradise. However, it did give me the traveling bug, and I knew that trip was just the beginning.

European Travel

On my honeymoon with Joel, we traveled to Europe, which included passage on a cruise ship for a few days. At every port of call, crew members told me that I better stay on the ship. Whenever I heard their unsolicited advice, I'd think, *I didn't come all this way to sit on the ship!*

As it turned out, Joel and I did fine. He pushed me in my wheelchair to see many of the sites. If there were sites I couldn't access, like the Acropolis, I just waited for Joel while he checked it out. When I waited at the bottom of the Acropolis, I sat in the sun and had fun people watching.

The trip to Italy and Greece would not have been doable without Joel. We walked often, but I also used my wheelchair. He pushed me all day over cobblestone streets, site seeing, stopping at spots for lunch or drinks, taking photos, or just people watching. Although I was sitting all day, by evening I was tired. Bouncing and jostling around in a wheelchair over cobblestones for hours made my butt sore. My knees were sore too, from sitting. Joel got a good workout, most definitely.

Usually, Joel and I got to the excursion sites on the cruise before the other members of our group. On our return to the ship, the crew seemed surprised because I told them all about our daily adventure. Their looks of surprise always pleased me.

During our European honeymoon, we took a cruise and one of our stops was Sorrento, a quaint village built on the sea cliffs overlooking the Bay of Naples in Southern Italy. We took a bus on the treacherous Amalfi Drive, carved out of the side of the coastal cliffs by the ancient

Romans. When we arrived, Joel and I sat in the town square, absorbed the incredible views, and observed the local culture, eating real pizza, and drinking Italian liqueurs like birra and limoncella.

Taormina, an ancient, small Sicilian town built on top of a cliff almost 400 years B.C.E. was a breathtaking highlight and well worth the journey. A bus dropped us off near the main square where we sat for a long time, soaking up the exquisite landscape and the sparkling luscious blues of the Ionian Sea. I wouldn't have missed that travel experience for anything!

We also visited Taormina's Amphitheatre ruins, an ancient, horseshoe-shaped Greek Theater carved from a natural rock hollow on a cliff overlooking panoramic vistas. Built by slaves, this was the stage for Greek music and drama, and later Roman Gladiator games. The historic ruins, the breathtaking view of surrounding mountains and ocean, and especially majestic Mt. Etna, are all etched in my memory.

A Second European Trip

By far, Joel was my easiest and funnest travel companion. He didn't bitch or complain. With rare exception, he was up for anything and any place. As travel partners, Joel did not think of me as a drag or a burden.

In 2009, Joel and I went on another European trip, this time to Italy, Amsterdam, and of course, Paris. A friend from high school joined us and again, people were amazed that I was traveling internationally. The rock band Green Day happened to be playing in Turin when we were visiting Italy, so we decided to go to the concert. It ended up being one of the greatest concerts I've ever been to, and I've been to many rock concerts in my lifetime. Singing along with some 30,000 enthusiastic Italians to rock songs in English. I'm not sure it gets

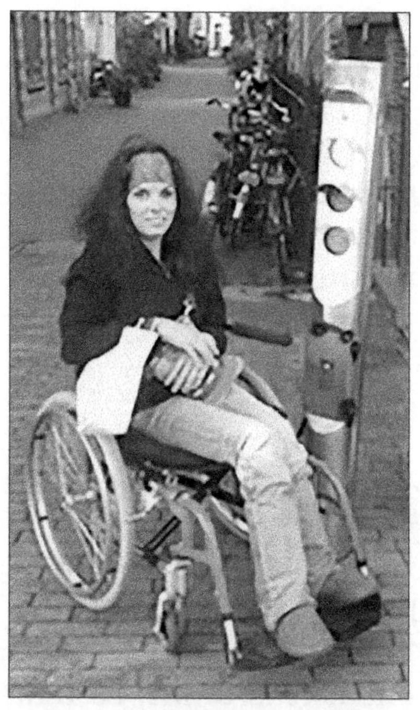

Teri in Amsterdam, 2010.

any better! Oh, and I must mention the handsome Italian man who carried me down the steps to my seat at the concert. Honestly, there are some benefits to not being able to manage steps!

In Paris, we rented an apartment right across the street from the building where Jim Morrison was found dead. Supposedly, our apartment was originally the apartment of the French artist Paul Cézanne. It's now owned by a Parisian who rents it to tourists. We went to the cemetery to see Jim Morrison's gravesite, which has a barricade around it. People still try to chip off pieces of his headstone, which has been replaced multiple times over the years.

On our way back from the cemetery, which was way on the other side of town from the apartment, we couldn't get a taxi. We stood in several taxi areas marked at spots on curbs, waiting. No cabs ever came. It started getting dark, and after hours of being pushed in my wheelchair on the cobble-stoned streets, my butt was so sore and numb. Several times I said, "Here's an idea, let's go into one of the hotels and have the front desk call us a taxi."

Everyone dismissed that idea and we kept walking in circles. The men I was with all had ideas that didn't work. Finally, I got them to go into a hotel, and we had a cab in 10 minutes.

When the cabby dropped us at the apartment, I asked him if he could pick us up at 4 a.m. the next morning for a ride to the airport. That way, we would avoid the problem of getting a taxi. It was a little difficult because of our language barrier, but the cabby and I got it after lots of hand gestures and laughing. The whole time I was negotiating our cab ride for the next morning, the guys were in the backseat hassling me, saying, "He'll never show up!"

When I got out of the cab, I told the cabby, "See you tomorrow!" Then I turned to the dumb boys and said, "Just you wait, he'll show!"

Sure enough, there was the cabby bright and early the next morning. With a big smile on my face, we got in the cab and I had a good laugh! I gave the cabby a great tip.

Oftentimes, I feel like no one listens to me, so that morning I felt vindicated. Plus, I was proud of my savvy for international traveling— a true pro!

European Spas

In 2010, Joel and I traveled to Europe for a third time, visiting Amsterdam in the Netherlands, Wuppertal and Hamburg in Germany, and then on to Paris. We traveled with the same friend and included my friend Peri from high school days. This was her first trip to Europe, so it was fun sharing adventures and seeing Peri appreciate everything so much. We went to a spa in Koln, Germany and another one in Amsterdam.

Oftentimes, U.S. tourists freak out at first when going to European spas. The spas are unisex, and everyone changes in the same locker room. In addition, the hot tubs, pools, and saunas are for nude soaking. Like my friend Peri said, "It's a good place to find a date because you already get to see what you will get."

Of course, we were checking things out at the spa as discreetly as possible, especially since the European spa scene was new to us. But Europeans don't think anything of it. No staring, no self-consciousness; people mind their own business, which is why I believe Europeans aren't as bold and invasive with me, asking inappropriate and personal questions about my body. Europeans don't ask, "What's your affliction? Did you know you have scars on your legs?"

I find Europeans much more discreet when it comes to sharing personal information.

Seeing the Sites

On this European jaunt we went to several tourist hot spots, including the Louvre, a boat ride down the Seine, and dinner at the top of the Eiffel Tower. No problems at all for me getting around to see the sites.

The Eiffel Tower was a great experience, despite the bad food. Taking the Tower's elevator was no problem in my wheelchair, other than it was packed, and not a good place to be if you are claustrophobic. The only problem on the crowded elevator was my sightline was even with people's butts or crotches.

Driving on the autobahn expressway was a blast and it didn't seem like we were going that fast until we looked at the speedometer. Keeping up with traffic required driving about 90 miles per hour. Like I said, I like going fast.

The Louvre was amazing, and I had zero problems getting around. We had a tour guide who showed us the three ladies: the *Mona Lisa,* the *Venus de Milo,* and *Winged Victory* (*Nike*). My favorite part of the Louvre was the exterior of the museum and its architecture. The October weather was extremely cold, so sitting in the wheelchair all day and not moving around made it feel colder. I kept hand warmers in my pockets and wore a hat.

Sometimes, parts of a trip that don't go perfectly are the most memorable and provide a good laugh later. I accept uncomfortableness or bathroom hassles. I don't let the inconveniences of a physical handicap bother me. I'm not a big complainer, just happy to be trekking the world. I accept my CP for what it is. This is my life—CP and all—I know no different.

This trip to Europe once again reminded me of how exciting it is to travel and visit foreign places. In my opinion, everyone should go to Europe before they die. As I write this, there are still many places I want to see.

Have to See It to Believe It

In Amsterdam, we stayed in an apartment near the house Rembrandt once lived in, or so we were told. We made a special trip to De Wallen, the largest, internationally known, red-light district in Amsterdam. This was quite a place to see. Very clean with many sex-oriented businesses and cafes offering an exciting nightlife. Hundreds of sex workers individually displayed their physical services in windows lit with red lights. We walked along some of the streets and saw women and men in the windows, in every human shape, size, color, and ethnicity. Shemales, or men with developed breasts who still had a penis were there, too. Clothing ran the gamut from French maid to dominatrix. There was something there for everyone.

The coffee shops in the red-light district allow people to purchase and smoke weed and cigarettes while sipping on coffee. Weed has been decriminalized in the Netherlands, but you cannot possess more than five grams for personal use. The government closely regulates the red-light district coffee shops. Mostly, tourists smoke weed in the shops.

The doorways to many public places in Amsterdam, like the coffee shops, are narrow. When I wanted to go into a coffee shop, I'd wheel up to the entrance, then stand up, and Joel or one of my friends would fold up my wheelchair to get it through the door. I walked in holding on to someone's hand or holding on to the doorjamb. Once inside, I'd sit in my chair, or a cafe chair at a table, or on a couch. If needed, my wheelchair was folded up somewhere near us. In one coffee shop, the bathroom was so small I could barely close the door, and my elbows touched the wall on either side of me. I'm petite, so you can imagine the size of the bathroom. My wheelchair sat outside the bathroom. While there, I wrote my initials and a message on the wall, along with the other comments written on that tiny bathroom's walls.

No photographs are allowed in the red-light district, so you must see it for yourself. Glad I was able to experience this famous district. I had heard people talk about it, so, to experience firsthand was interesting, to say the least!

Hamburg's Reeperbahn

In Hamburg, I saw the famous, German, hard rock band, Scorpions, first formed in 1966. I had forgotten how many Scorpions' songs I knew. At the time, it was supposed to be their last concert, claiming they were going to retire; but we all know how many bands say that. Despite ongoing breakup rumors, in July 2025 the Scorpions celebrated 60 years of band history and of course, their concert in Hamburg was recorded for a live album! Thrilled that I got to witness this historic band on their home turf.

The Reeperbahn is a street in Hamburg that is the city's red-light district and one of Hamburg's two nightlife centers. Reeperbahn makes Amsterdam's red-light district seem like Disneyland. It's called the most sinful mile in the world—and I have been there!

Teri and Claus in NYC on their way to Europe via an ocean liner, 2025.

Now, don't get the idea that I go to all these cities just to see all the seedy sex places, but they are a part of what I'm interested in seeing. Reeperbahn is the heart of the sex shops, along with night clubs, restaurants, and bars. I'm talking sex shows of all kinds. One club with a marquee on the awning advertised "Bar Bistro Restaurant Travestie-Show Pulverfass Cabaret." I assumed Travestie Show is transvestite. I'm not sure about Pulverfass Cabaret, but it must've been good.

When I saw the sign, I said to my friends, "Look, one stop shopping!"

We stayed at Hotel Pacific, which is famous because the Beatles stayed there before they were the Beatles. In the early 1960s, the Beatles played clubs in Reeperbahn for two years before they found fame.

While there, we visited Beatlemania, a museum dedicated to the history of the Beatles. It was located near Beatles-Platz, a plaza built in 2008 to commemorate Hamburg's importance in early Beatle history. The plaza is painted black to resemble a vinyl record, and five metal statues surround the plaza: John Lennon, Paul McCartney, George Harrison, Stuart Sutcliffe, and a hybrid of Pete Best and Ringo Starr. Each of these people played with the Beatles during their gigs on Reeperbahn. Sadly, the private museum closed in June 2012 due to lack of interest and hard economic times.

More Travel Plans

My plan is to continue traveling for many years to come, as long as I can. I don't want to look back on my life as an old woman—if I get old—and have regrets. Right now, I'm packing for a return trip to Europe. My bucket list includes the following:

- Go to Africa on a safari.
- Go to Borneo and see the endangered orangutans at Camp Leaky, a refuge run by anthropologist and leading orangutan authority, Dr. Birutė Galdikas. I want to hold a baby orangutan.
- Last, but not least, meet Steven Tyler, the lead singer of Aerosmith.

Many steps to reach the Buddha, Thailand, 2021.

Chapter 25
The Ups and Downs of Travel

Now that I have shared my love of traveling, I must share that there were difficult experiences. Still, I wouldn't want to miss the excitement and fun of traveling, but there are those times when it was just too much. I am sharing a couple of experiences here to give you some understanding of what it is like for people with disabilities trying to travel. And if you have physical disabilities, you will know what I'm talking about!

Unexpected Challenges

Sometimes, travelling is not easy. Things can happen, like losing a screw from my walker. Overseas, there aren't always standards that are met for people with disabilities. To be fair, the standards in the United States aren't the best either, even though people like to think so. To me, it's not much different than things I encounter in daily life. I make do with what I have. People can be helpful, too. When on vacation, most people seem to be in a good mood. So, when I need it, I accept help, but I do like to be as independent as possible. Asking does not come easy for me.

Wherever I travel, the bathroom situation is an ongoing challenge—whether in the United States or internationally. I don't let it stop me from doing anything, but I make decisions differently based on the circumstances. The biggest worry I have is accessible bathrooms. When I find one and surprisingly, more often than not, I am relieved in more ways than one.

If getting to the bathroom looks like it's going to be a pain in the ass, I try not to drink a lot during the outing. Or I seek out other alternatives, like outside in a discreet area where I can relieve myself. If I am outdoors on a motorcycle or camping trip, I find a spot where I have something to lean on or hold onto, and squat, and go. However, I have a confession: I pee outside when I need to. Shyness and Modesty are not my middle names. As I like to say, "You gotta do what ya gotta do." I know I'm not the only one!

When flying, I love airplane bathrooms because they are small and close by. Walking down the plane's aisle, I can hold on to the top of seats, which makes for easy navigating. Once inside the bathroom, I have plenty of things to hold on to. Obviously, the closer my plane seat is to the bathroom, the better.

Airport Security

In all my travels, getting patted down at the airport is inevitably an interesting experience. Oftentimes crazy, unpredictable, and humiliating stuff goes on. One time in particular, I was at Portland Airport (PDX) on my way to Reno for my niece Alix's college graduation. As usual, I was patted down because I don't walk through the x-ray scanner for humans.

Getting patted down is always different. You would think TSA would have a standard protocol for people in wheelchairs, or with walkers or canes. On this pat down, a female TSA agent was very thorough. During the TSA check, she complimented me on my looks several times. The agent had me turn my palms up to swab them and then put them through the machine that analyzes everything, especially minute residue from explosives. The machine beeped, indicating there was a problem.

Another agent came over and said TSA would have to take me to a private room and give me a more thorough pat down. The original agent and the new agent went with me to the private room. They patted me down again, this time with an open hand, which is normally done with the back of the palm in sensitive areas. However, they used the front of their hands, which made me feel extremely uncomfortable. While the first agent was patting down my crotch area, she told me how pretty I was. They also unpacked my bag and thoroughly checked it. They asked what I had put on my hands that morning. I said, “Chanel anti-wrinkle cream.”

The agents responded, “Cosmetics and creams can have the same properties as explosives.”

Unlike the United States, in Europe my airport security pat downs were no big deal. They basically patted down my arms and said, “You’re good.”

I think European security agents have a better understanding of who is a legitimate threat and who is not. The U.S. airport agents are reactionary or play defense more than planning an offense. It seems to me that people in the United States overreact to everything after something happens.

When TSA started making people take their shoes off, I was pissed. Me and shoes—although I love them—have a difficult time. It takes me a long time to get shoes on. When airport security agents started asking me to take my shoes off, I said, “I will if you can put them back on.”

One TSA supervisor asked, “Why don’t you wear something like flip flops, which you can take on and off easily?”

I thought about telling the agent why I can't wear slip-on shoes but decided against it since I was trying to catch a flight. However, the main reason I can't wear slip-on shoes is because I have no muscle in my feet. If someone waved a million dollars in my face, saying this is yours if you wiggle your toes, I'd try with all my might, but I'd have to pass. If I wore flip flops, I would have to physically separate my toes to place them on my feet. I can't point my feet. All the shoes I put on must be manually manipulated to get my foot in.

Sandals are no good because they don't give me enough support and my foot slides all over. Not to mention, I am self-conscious about my feet. I have skin and nail problems that developed in my early twenties after a trip to the Oregon coast. Since then, I have been unable to clear it up. According to doctors, my skin condition is exasperated by bad circulation from my calves down. I love boots and wear them the most, even with shorts because they cover up my calves. When I find shoes that are easier than usual to put on, I stick with them.

Transported Like Cattle

The most jarring experience I had on an international trip happened at the Athens airport. In 1996, disabled passengers were transported to the airplane in a stunningly archaic manner. Basically, Joel and I were separated because he was not allowed to ride with me in the back of a truck used to transport people in wheelchairs. The set up was so bizarre, Joel thought he may never see me again. Before I was loaded in the truck, Joel whispered, "What the fuck?"

The truck resembled a U-Haul with no windows, just plywood on all sides. I was told to hang on to a strap that attached to the inside of the truck. When they opened the back of the truck, I could see other passengers hanging on to straps while their wheelchairs moved around, unsecured. People had blank stares on their faces, as if in shock. It felt like we were third class citizens.

An attendant from the airline wheeled me up the ramp and closed the overhead door. It was pitch black, smelled like plywood, and the whole scene was horribly dehumanizing as we rumbled along the airport road. Off we went like animals to slaughter. I was so happy to see the blue Greek sky once the door was opened. The ride only took about 10 minutes, but it seemed a lot longer. Riding in the dark, unable to see where we were going, I imagined Jews being transported in cattle cars to Nazi concentration camps during World War II, and what must've been going through their minds. I kept thinking, *It's the 1990s for fuck's sake, is this the best idea the airlines can come up with? Really?*

Once the truck got to the plane, they wheeled me off. I got out of my chair and walked up the airplane stairs, holding on to the railing.

One of the reasons I like to travel is to experience how others live—but this one in Athens was beyond the pale. That was more than 25 years ago, so I hope the Athens airport has developed a better system by now. Experiences like this make me grateful for U.S. standards that push for accessibility for the physically disabled. The ADA is not perfect, by far, but it sure makes it a little easier for the physically handicapped than some other countries.

The V.I.P. Treatment

On an up note, travel for disabled people seems to have improved quite a bit in the United States and Europe. On my second international trip in 2009, I was relieved to not be shuttled around an airport like cattle in a box truck. At all the European airports an attendant facilitated my airport needs, whisking my traveling companions and me through all the long lines. We got to the front of every line, making it through security in minutes. We even got our own room in an airport lounge, stocked with snacks and drinks. When a connecting flight arrived, the attendant came and escorted us to our next gate. This time, I felt like a VIP rather than a third-class citizen. My friends soon learned that sometimes there are advantages to traveling with me!

On a recent West Coast flight, I was upgraded to first class because my seat was in the back of the plane. Of course, I took advantage of the first-class service and I had three vodka tonics. After serving me a couple drinks, the flight attendant said, "I just need to say, you are really put together sister."

He liked my outfit; a tight fitting, short, cream-colored Bebe dress with my new, distressed-brown Frye boots. I had dreadlocks at the time, and they were all down and messy, and I had a cream-colored, leather-studded hairband. I knew I looked good, and I appreciated the compliment.

Then, an older man got up to use the bathroom and asked me, "Are you a celebrity?"

I laughed and told him, "No, not the last time I looked."

The guy across from me joined the conversation, adding, "You get that all the time, don't you?"

"Never!" I said.

After the flurry of compliments, I decided I should wear that outfit more often. By the time I got off that flight, I was in fine spirits, feeling confident and beautiful, happy to be traveling.

Chapter 26
Seeking Thrills and Chills

Over the years, I have done many things that people seem amazed by, assuming I don't do physical activities because I have a disability. When they express their astonishment, I wonder, *What am I supposed to do? Sit in the house, eat bonbons, and watch TV?*

Whenever I tell people about my international travels or my physical activity, they say, "Wow, you get around!" I have an adventurous spirit and trying new things and challenging myself are a big part of enjoying my life.

Bungee Jumping

For my thirtieth birthday in 1994, my co-workers gave me a gift certificate to go bungee jumping. This was something I had wanted to do for a long time but couldn't find anyone who was willing to work with me. The day I cashed in on my gift, about 30 friends and co-workers joined me for the adventure. Some of my family members came, too, including my mom. Nana and Bapa decided not to come because, as Nana explained, "I did not spend all that time teaching you to walk so you could go jump off a bridge!"

My dad offered to pay me $100 not to go. I told him, "It cost me $100 to go, so you will have to up your price."

The owner of Bungee Masters, Casey Dale, organizes jumps from an old, private, logging bridge in Chelatchie

Bungee jumping, 1994.

Prairie, Washington, located about 40 miles north of Portland. Today, Bungee Masters still organizes outrageous bungee jumps, including from helicopters. For years, Casey has worked with Oregon and insurance companies to successfully maintain high safety standards for bungee jumpers. So, I was in good hands!

We all crowded onto the narrow bridge with a guardrail only on one side. About 200 feet below was a sparkling river with Class V rapids rushing and swirling about. I wasn't especially scared, mostly just eager to get going.

When Casey asked who would be jumping, I was the only one in the group to raise my hand. He laughed. There was a weight requirement of at least 90 pounds, and I only weighed in the mid-80s. Casey got around the weight issue easily by tying four bungee cords, bundled together with strips of Velcro, around my waist. I needed the extra weight so I would bounce at the end of the jump and not just go straight down. When someone heavy jumps, the bridge shakes—but that was not my problem!

When I was ready to jump, Casey held me by the harness strap around my torso and lifted me over the railing on to the wooden ledge. After a "one, two, three" count, he let go and I jumped. My mom said, "You looked more like a leaf falling."

At first, I couldn't feel the extra weight of the bungee cords on me, so for a split second I thought, *I've come unhooked!* That was the only moment when I was scared.

Then I flew with the biggest adrenaline rush I had ever experienced, laughing all the way down. It was a clear, sunny, sparkling day—the kind of day you wait for in the usually gray, rainy, Pacific Northwest. I didn't realize how high the bridge really was—about 20 stories—until I saw the video. I jumped twice that day; first forward off the platform, and then backward. The backwards jump is called "Elevator to Hell" because it is considered the scariest. However, I thought the forward jump was way scarier, maybe because it was my first jump.

Afterward, we went for drinks. For two days after that experience, my heart was beating so fast I could almost see it pounding through my chest. As far as life experiences go, it was amazing. After my bungee jumping, I called Nana to let her know I survived.

Exactly one year later, I bungee jumped again. Casey said the previous year he didn't think I had gotten the full feeling of jumping since I can't really jump from a standing position. The second time, he went out on the wooden ledge with me, hooked himself to the bridge, picked me up, and threw me off the bridge! That time was even more fun, and even more scary. Casey explained, "The first time, you didn't know what you were getting into. This time, you realized how crazy it is to jump off a bridge!"

Teri skydiving in 2020.

Skydiving

For a long time I wanted to try skydiving. But like everything else that involves risk, I had to talk someone into working with me to make it possible. Unfortunately, I can't just walk in and sign up for the adventure. Because of my CP, people usually find reasons to not let me try something physically demanding.

Several years ago, I found a skydiving outfit about an hour from Portland, and I called to see if they would work with me. I told them I had CP and explained my physical challenges. Their response was, "Sure, come out, we'll evaluate you."

I went out on a Saturday afternoon thinking I'd be out there for quite a while because they said to allow most of the afternoon. When I got there, I walked into the office dressed in shorts, a t-shirt, and boots. A woman who worked there looked at me from head to toe for maybe 30 seconds and said, "Oh no, you can't go."

I asked, "What about the "evaluation?"

Well, there was no evaluation. She didn't even give me a chance. "You have to be able to climb the ladder into the plane," she explained.

Again, I mentioned that the man I talked to on the phone said he would give me an evaluation if I came out. That didn't seem to matter to this woman. I left that skydiving business fucking pissed off. Once again, I felt judged and held back because of my CP, not given a chance to prove what I can do. That day, it seemed like everything was a fight and it would take more planning, or I would have to prove I can do something. I told myself, *Eventually, I will go skydiving. It might take time, but, one day, I will do it.*

That day finally came.

Valentine's Day 2020, Claus surprised me with a Valentine's card that said, "You are going skydiving today!" When I read the card, I asked in disbelief, "Today?"

Claus and I, along with his friend Markus, drove to San Diego Skydive. It was special having Markus join us since he is a speed skydiver from Switzerland. When we got there, I met my instructor, Victor, who could not have been a better fit for me. We immediately hit it off and I was relieved that he wasn't nervous around me, at all. After an hour or so of instruction and getting suited up, we got on the plane, which I thought looked old and rickety,

As we climbed up to our desired altitude, about 13,500 feet, I sat on Victor's lap so he could strap me to the front of his torso. The plane was filled with other jumpers and everyone was oddly quiet. To break the spell, I clapped my hands and said loudly, "Come on! Is everyone excited? We are jumping out of a plane!"

They all laughed, then everyone seemed to relax a bit. When it was time, the first duo jumped and then it was our turn. I thought we would've stopped at the door for a moment and Victor would've said something. Instead, with no hesitation, Victor just stepped out the plane door seconds after the first jumper. We went into free fall for one minute. I hardly ever use the word epic, but that's what came to mind. After one minute, which seemed so long, Victor pulled the cord and we gently floated up as the parachute opened. Victor had a wrist camera on his left wrist and asked me how I liked it as we drifted down. With a gigantic smile, I said, "It's fucking epic!"

Once the parachute opened, the trip down seemed to take longer than I imagined. Victor pointed out various areas of San Diego as we gently floated toward earth. It was as if we were just sharing a beer and looking at the scenery. We landed smoothly and effortlessly, and my feet didn't even touch the ground.

For at least a week, my adrenaline was pumping, and I had a permanent grin on my face. It felt like I couldn't close my lips, completely transformed by the experience. For a long time afterward, I thought skydiving could be a cure for depression. If you feel down, go jump out of a plane. There's *nothing* like it.

About a week later, I got the skydiving video via email. Markus watched it with us and he said I had perfect form. I giggled. "I don't think anyone has told me that about anything I've done in my life, Markus."

He gave me one of his speed skydiving shirts for my efforts. I had arrived! By far the best Valentine Day's gift Claus ever gave me, and the most memorable.

Motorcycle Trips

In recent years, I have had the thrill of traveling with Claus on his motorcycle. It feels as if a whole new world has opened for me. All my life, I have liked moving fast and the feeling of zooming down the road on a sunny day is unbeatable. I love riding motorcycles, or for that matter, doing anything that gets my adrenaline going.

Teri, Claus, and their ride.

In 2012, I took my first long motorcycle ride from San Diego to a tiny town in Arizona. For six hours, Claus and I zoomed down the highway on his Harley and we didn't even stop once to pee. I felt so free, I just wanted to keep going. Claus said I was amazing, which means I wasn't a pain in the ass to a lifelong biker.

The only thing I noticed when Claus took me off the bike was it took a minute to straighten out my left leg because it had been bent for so long. He had bungeed my feet to the bike pegs because my feet slipped off due to a lack of muscle control. Aside from a brief leg stiffness, that trip was a highlight for my adventurous spirit.

On that bike ride I felt good about myself for the first time in a long time. After several long motorcycle trips, I no longer need a bungee cord to hold my feet in place. Progress!

Sturgis

Since then, I have been to Sturgis, South Dakota five times with Claus. All his friends have accepted me graciously, and now, they are my buddies. They make me feel like a part of their group, Camp 50. This is the name they gave the group that comes to Sturgis every year. It's a campsite called Wild Bill's, outside Deadwood, South Dakota. Campsite #50 is reserved every year, and most of the members have Camp 50 tattoos, but not me, yet.

Claus's friend Meyer, a 90-year-old man with a long, red-graying beard, warned Claus, "Whenever there is a ride coming up, don't bother coming without Teri."

When Meyer and I first met, he said something that made me immediately like him. When I got out of the truck, Claus grabbed my walker from the truck bed. He handed it to me and Meyer said to Claus without missing a beat, "Oh look, finally one you can catch."

Once at camp, Claus told Meyer, "You're going to outlive me." Meyer looked at me, winked, and said with a laugh, "That's what I'm hoping."

We took the southern route to Sturgis in both 2014 and 2015. Leaving from San Diego, we rode through Arizona, Utah, Colorado, Wyoming, and finally, South Dakota. My favorite parts were riding through Monument Valley and the beautiful, red rock formations in Utah. We stayed at the San Juan Inn

Monument Valley.

built in the side of the rocks at Mexican Hat, Utah, on the San Juan River.

Colorado was another of my favorite places. We took backroads 95 percent of the time. Riding through farm country with rushing rivers was magnificent, unlike anything I had ever seen. Every time I see that kind of landscape, I talk about moving there.

In Colorado, I met Claus's friends, Greg and Peggy, a couple who have been together for all their adult lives and are genuinely happy to spend every day in each other's company. I liked them immediately because we are like-minded. In many ways. Greg is a well-known tattoo artist who retired from his business that had been going strong since 1982. Now, he tattoos women's areolas after they've had a mastectomy for breast cancer. Good people. Greg gave me a tattoo on my arm with a compass pointing NW with faded continents in the background, along with his colorful signature flowers. I feel he captured a part of my essence in this tattoo.

On our motorcycle trips to Sturgis we have had great weather and no mechanical problems. Claus has a 2003 Ultra Classic Electra Glide anniversary edition Harley. He says it's because I'm traveling with the best road captain. He knows what he's doing, and I appreciate that he is watches closely for weather changes. If it looks like rain, we find an out-of-the-way motel and hangout in whatever little town we discover. When the weather clears, we pull out early in the morning and head on down the road to our next destination. The feeling of being on the open road and spontaneous is unbeatable.

In Wyoming, we hung out at the Eagles Nest Tavern where Sturgis riders usually converge on the way there, and back. On my first visit to the tavern, I got exceptionally wasted because "newbies" do shots. I remember barely anything about that day. On the way back, we stopped at the tavern again, and the owner told me I was famous. Apparently, people were coming in asking about me and wondered when I'd be back.

Of course, people were interested to know how I did on such a long trip, about 3,800 miles. Claus assured them that I was no problem, at all. Claus gained a lot of respect for me after that arduous round journey trip on the back of his motorcycle. As I've said before, I am up for adventure.

We ran into a lot of trailer-bikers, which is a big "no-no" around the group I was with. They make fun of people who trailer their bikes and just ride once they hit Sturgis, especially when they come from just a state away. Claus and I rode all the way from Southern California. He told me, "You are no poser, and you have the heart of a true biker!"

I have been on many rides since. It's one of my favorite things to do. Hopefully, I can continue to take motorcycle trips for years to come.

Chapter 27

Do's & Don'ts for the "Normals"

I want to share some do's and don'ts to help those of you who may find it difficult to communicate or relate to someone with a disability. My feelings about certain events in my life, or things that have been said to me, have profoundly shaped my self-perception as well as my perception about many things. The uninvited opinions and feelings from others about my disability have really messed with my thoughts. So, listen up!

Do Not Say or Ask This!

For starters, when you come upon someone who is on some kind of wheels and you'd like to meet them, don't lead with "What's your affliction?"

Do say, "Nice to meet you" or "Hi, what's your name?"

Do not talk to an adult with a physical disability in a baby voice or pat them on the head. It's condescending. Do speak to them in an age-appropriate manner.

If you think the person on wheels is hot, do not say, "You are pretty (or handsome) for a crippled person," or "You are hot, too bad you can't walk."

Do say, "You are pretty or handsome," or whatever compliment you want to share.

Leave the other part of the sentence out! It's a much better compliment without a "but." Definitely do not ask, "Can you have sex?"

If a person with a physical disability decides you're hot, too, then maybe you'll find out. If not, just let it go. In that situation, honestly, it's none of your business.

Do not refer to the person with a physical disability as "a piece of equipment." For example, someone yells, "Here comes a wheelchair, move out of the way."

Do say, "Please move. This person is trying to get by." They will see the chair—unless they are blind.

When you are amazed that someone with a disability can do things like everyone else on the planet, do keep your jaw from dropping open. Try to think of what your response would be if you were talking to any other normal or able-bodied person.

Do not point out a physically disabled person's imperfections, such as scars. Trust me, everyone knows they have scars. I don't go around saying, "Hey, you're ugly!" or "Did you know you have moles all over your face?" or "You're fat."

Get the picture?

Listen

Do listen when a person with disabilities is talking to you. Do not assume if someone is physically handicapped, they are also mentally impaired. Does Stephen Hawking, the brilliant physicist and best-selling author, ring a bell? I rest my case.

If this is too hard to do, my best advice is to think before you speak. If you don't, you may end up in a book like this.

People are people, whether they are sitting in a wheelchair or standing up. Just treat them like you'd treat anyone else. Same goes if they are being an asshole. Tell them they are being an asshole, even if they're sitting in a wheelchair. Nothing like feeling you fit in with everyone else, right?

I hope that able-bodied people understand that people in wheelchairs are not necessarily mentally challenged. Do not treat them as if they don't have a life of their own, complete with thoughts, feelings, dreams. Remember Stephen Hawkings.

In recent years, many wounded soldiers have come home from the wars in Iraq and Afghanistan, dealing with incredible physical challenges. The number of disabled veterans continues to increase, and their growing numbers will demand that they be treated more respectfully and as part of mainstream society. These wounded veterans are adjusting to a new way of life and will probably experience many of the questions and assumptions that I do. Hopefully there will eventually be a better understanding that people with disabilities are just like everyone else.

Appropriate Office Behavior

Working in an office opens another arena filled with people asking insensitive questions and saying inappropriate things. Their curiosity often quickly leads them to foot-in-mouth disease. When people first met me at BPA, the first thing they usually said was something about my physical condition, or my mode of transportation, whether I was using a walker, a wheelchair, or a scooter. They seemed unable to simply introduce themselves and say, "Hi, nice to meet you," like they would if meeting anyone else. Almost daily, people at work called me Mario Andretti or they jumped in front of me, joking that they wanted me to hit them so they could collect workman's comp. It was all playful, but not so funny after a couple decades. It became old and boring. If people had come up with new material, perhaps I would've been more impressed.

A co-worker once said to me, "Do you have someone do your make up and put together your clothes every day?"

I said, "Yes, I do—it's me!"

She said, "You always look so good and well put together."

I tried to make light of it, so I responded, "I wish I had my own wardrobe and makeup person."

Actually, I am good at clothes and makeup. Those are an important part of how I present myself to the world.

When you meet someone with a physical disability, don't ask them "What's wrong with you?"

It's offensive and honestly, it's none of your business, and certainly not appropriate when you have a casual exchange with a stranger. First, you need to get to know a person, share your own life and shortcomings, and then you have that conversation with your friend, if they are willing.

Throughout my life, I have chosen certain people as my friends because when we met their opening line wasn't, "Hey, what's your condition?" or "What's wrong with you?"

Instead, my friends treated me as a person they cared about—not a condition to comment on. My friends didn't talk to me in a baby voice like people often do. They are comfortable knowing me and being with me. They accept me just as I am. Those friends are hard to find.

Nothing Is "Wrong" with Me!

In 2013, I went with Claus on my first motorcycle run called the Yuma Prison Run. It was at the Yuma fairgrounds and people came from all over the country on their bikes. There were campsites and booths selling food, motorcycle clothes, and jewelry, along with rock bands, a bike show, and anything else that might interest your average biker. There were hardcore biker club types, families, and just average people who have been riding for years. Everybody meets at these runs to have fun and to bullshit with old friends.

With so many people around, it's inevitable that some will ask me questions about what they call "my condition." The Yuma Run was no exception. I met a couple, Candy and Phil, who are acquaintances with people in the group we camped with. They were sitting around the circle of lawn chairs set up at camp, staring at me intently. I know when people are doing that—they can barely wait to ask me the big question.

"What's wrong with you?" Phil asked.

Very matter-of-factly I explained that I have CP and it affected my legs at birth. However, later I regretted telling Phil. I hate when that's the very first question people think to ask me. It's rude. It would've been like me asking Phil straight up, just by looking at his strange demeanor, "What's wrong with you?"

This is an example of people who don't look so good themselves, or behave oddly, or seem emotionally distraught, thinking they can just ask me what's wrong with *me* because of my physical disability. It's as if I'm open game.

Then, Phil's girlfriend, Candy, sitting about 15 feet across from me, said, "Oh, so cerebral palsy...but you are feeling good, right"?

I half expected her to throw a blanket over my frail legs! "I feel fine, I'm not dying."

The entire weekend, when Phil and Candy spoke to me, it was in a tender voice. I couldn't help but wonder, *Do they think I am breakable?*

When someone asks me what's wrong with me, I usually have to stop and think about what's wrong. I may think, *Do I have food on my face or something?*

Should I start asking people, "What's wrong with you?" before introducing myself. I bet there's more wrong with the people asking me that question—far beyond my having CP.

Normal Conversation, Please

On that same trip, Claus and I met a family from Lake Havasu. They were nice, but the uncle could not shut up about his friend in a wheelchair and how badly he wanted to build him a wheelchair. It was nice that he was wanting to build a chair, but I wasn't that interested in details. It felt as if the uncle couldn't think of anything else to talk about with me.

I just want people to understand there is more to my life, more to me, and more subjects I am interested in and able to talk about beyond my disability. By the end of our meeting, after some beers, he handed his card to Claus, saying, "Call me if you'd like me to build her a chair."

Wonder why he didn't just ask me! I was sitting there, too.

On the other hand, this obnoxious uncle's grown niece was sweet and kind. We had a nice conversation, shared stories, and learned about each other. She told me she just got a divorce from her wife. I said, "I did that too, but a guy!" We both laughed.

Our conversation felt normal; a sharing back and forth about our lives with no mention of my disability or wheelchair, or what's wrong with me! In turn, there wasn't a big focus on the fact that she is lesbian.

How nice to be approached first with something other than any variation of "What's wrong...."

Chapter 28

Final Thoughts

I have not been to a psychiatrist or psychologist to specifically talk about my core feelings of having cerebral palsy (CP), even though I am sure some of my insecurities stem from that. I have been to counselors to talk about work stresses, the death of my grandparents, relationships ending, and fears about new relationships, but not just my CP. While I have not been depressed because I was born with CP, I have been scared about figuring out my life as a single person, my independence, caring for myself, and the prospect of being alone. Not sure these issues are much different than what able-bodied people discuss in therapy. I see myself the same as any other person.

My disability is a factor in most relationships, at some level, but I am used to it, and I deal with it. If the relationship works out, great! If someone puts up resistance because I have CP, then I move on. Sometimes, the moving on part takes me awhile. If anything, I think I give too many chances to a partner, or I hope they will change their behavior, and they don't. That is the problem. Unfortunately, it usually doesn't happen, and I eventually leave.

No Apologies

My CP is a part of who I am, and I accept that. What I want in my life is for others to see me as a whole person, and accept me just the way I am, including the fact that I have CP.

It's been pointed out to me that I say "sorry'" a lot—even for things that I know aren't my fault. If someone is waiting for me, I say, "Sorry." If it takes me a long time to do something, I say, "Sorry." If I pass by someone, I say, "Sorry." When I got on the train every day to go to work, and people moved for me, I said, "Sorry." I've noticed I am constantly apologizing for my life. I really wish I would stop it.

When I hear myself say, "Sorry," I instantly think, *Why am I saying sorry? I didn't do anything.*

Perhaps I'm apologizing for being an inconvenience. I worry, *Am I holding them up? Or am I in the way?*

I also realize this compulsion to say "I'm sorry" is problematic for women in general. It's like we must apologize for having needs or being inconvenient or taking up space. It's a double whammy when you're a woman and you have a disability.

So, sorry—not sorry!

Embracing My Life

When I first met Claus, he told me, "Most people are paralyzed from the neck up." That made me belly laugh. It's true, I just hadn't thought of it like that.

Many times, I have been asked if I was able to walk normally tomorrow, would I want that? The answer might be, Yes! Although, when I think about it, it scares me. I have had CP since I was born, it's a part of my being. I know how to live my life in my body, just as it is. If I suddenly was able-bodied, I would have to relearn everything. One thing I know for sure: If I could, I would disappear and travel with a backpack for as long as I wanted. I wouldn't have to wait for an invitation. I'd be gone!

If I could walk effortlessly, yes, everyday shit would be easier, however, I think I'm fine how I am. You don't miss what you don't know. For instance, I didn't miss not having my dad around when I was young because I didn't know him until I was in the sixth grade. However, I always had Bapa—he's the one who got my Father's Day cards.

While physically I may be slow and not the one to help move furniture, when it comes to intellectual or emotional support, people in my life seek me out. Claus says I'm like the "godfather" of the family, or should I say godmother! Others often ask, "What does Teri think?"

I have great skills for organizing, planning, researching, remembering, or being a sounding board for problem solving. And when needed, I've offered financial support. What I lack in physical prowess, I more than make up for in all other aspects of life skills. Growing up, my father regularly turned to me for my perspective or advice about family. My reputation in the family is being the smart one, the one who's got her shit together. So, you see, there are great advantages to not being so good at things like mopping, vacuuming, yardwork, or helping people move!

Most of my life I've been happy, and I've had many interesting and fun experiences. I've done things that many people never get a chance to do. I've traveled internationally, I've had a good job, I've had the money to buy houses and invest, and I've been married and divorced and loved again. I want people to understand that I am normal. Like everyone else, I'm figuring out my life with all its ups and downs.

With most things, the only difference is that physically I'm slower and getting older. It takes me longer to put

Teri in Phuket, Thailand, 2021.

on my shoes, and bending over to pick things up takes longer. But as the comedian George Burns once said, “You know you’re getting old when you stoop to tie your shoelaces and wonder what else you could do while you’re down there.” I think getting older, with all its challenges, is standard fare for most of us.

People will learn patience with me, if they choose to hang around long enough. But really, what’s the hurry? Unless the house is burning down, is there really a problem with taking it slower?

I Am Who I Am

My upbringing, my family, my environment, and all the things I've done, and I still want to do, are what make me, me. The way things are in my life, that is what was meant to be. The way I handle them is what makes me who I am. The good and the bad are all a part of me. There's nothing particularly heroic or superhuman about me living with CP.

I am a regular person at peace overall with my body, yet society judges me as if I'm trapped in a body they decide is not normal or acceptable. Maybe one of my life lessons is to not get wrapped up in others' judgments about my body and feel like I have to prove I am a regular woman. I am happy with my life and how I have handled most of my challenges.

My hope is that the rest of the world can see people like me and grow to understand that the only difference is the way each of us perceives the world and moves through it. Everything else, every feeling, is pretty much how most other people are, too.

Not everything I do should be thought of as strong or inspiring. I am just living my life, and I want friends, fun, and adventures like most people. Give people a chance or an opportunity to become more and achieve more than what is expected of them, and they probably will. Each of us must figure out how to grab our life and live it to the fullest. That's what I'm doing.

Like Nana told me many times, "I wish I could go back to those doctors and show them what a vegetable you turned out to be."

I do, too, Nana.

MICHAEL PEARCE

About the Author

TERI SIRI and her twin sister were born prematurely in Portland, Oregon in September 1964. After several months it became clear that Teri's physical development was not on par with her twin, Traci. After she was nine months old, doctors diagnosed Teri with spastic cerebral palsy (CP), a physical condition that affects her legs and muscle stiffness.

Despite dire predictions from the experts that Teri would most likely be a "vegetable" and should be institutionalized, Teri's family fully embraced her and treated her as "normal." Teri's maternal grandparents, Nana and Bapa, were key people in her life, along with her mom and sisters, as she endured multiple surgeries, rehab, and daily challenges living with CP.

As a young adult, Teri moved to Portland, Oregon, in part to be near her Nana and Bapa, but also to establish her independence. Eventually, Teri got a job with Bonneville Power Administration (BPA) in Portland. Over the years, she had high-responsibility jobs, including a Scheduler. In this high-pressure position, Teri bought and sold electric power hourly in what is called "real time." This job was similar, in many ways, to working on the stock market, but buying and selling electrical power. After 24 years at BPA, she retired.

Teri has lived a full and adventurous life and continues to do so. She has fallen in love several times, married, divorced, worked, and retired. She has traveled internationally several times, bought a car and learned to drive, purchased homes, and has been financially independent throughout her adult life. Any activity that someone declared off limits for Teri because of CP, Teri would accomplish, proving the naysayer wrong.

After Teri retired from BPA, she moved back to San Diego in 2012 to be closer to her family. She also fell in love again and has been with her partner ever since. Together, they regularly take extended, cross-country motorcycle trips. Teri describes in her book the incredible freedom of speeding down a beautiful country road, feeling the wind on her face.

Teri writes, "I like anything that gets my adrenaline pumping," which has inspired her to go bungee jumping, skydiving, snow skiing, sailing, and more. She also loves music, especially Steven Tyler and Aerosmith, and has attended many rock concerts in different venues, including Italy and Germany.

Currently, Teri and her partner, Claus, live in their country home just east of San Diego. This is Teri's first book.

Visit her website at:
www.prettyforacrippledgirl.com
or email teri@prettyforacrippledgirl.com

www.ingramcontent.com/pod-product-compliance
Lightning Source LLC
Jackson TN
JSHW080844211225
95654JS00001B/1

* 9 7 8 0 9 3 9 1 6 5 8 4 1 *